W9-ASH-436

COLD WAR AND COMMON SENSE

D843
W47

COLD WAR AND COMMON SENSE

A Close Look at the Record of Communist Gains and Failures and of Freedom's Fortunes in the Mid-Twentieth Century

by

THOMAS W. WILSON, Jr.

77178

NEW YORK GRAPHIC SOCIETY
GREENWICH, CONNECTICUT
1962

JAN 1963

LIBRARY OF CONGRESS CATALOG CARD NO. 62–13308

©THOMAS W. WILSON, JR., 1962

ALL RIGHTS RESERVED. NO PART OF THIS BOOK MAY BE REPRODUCED IN ANY FORM WITHOUT PERMISSION IN WRITING FROM THE PUBLISHER, EXCEPT BY A REVIEWER WHO MAY QUOTE BRIEF PASSAGES IN A REVIEW TO BE PRINTED IN A MAGAZINE OR NEWSPAPER.

GRATEFUL ACKNOWLEDGMENT IS GIVEN TO:
HARPER & BROTHERS FOR PERMISSION TO QUOTE FROM *Protracted Conflict* BY ROBERT STRAUSZ-HUPÉ, AND OTHERS; REYNAL & COMPANY, INC., FOR PERMISSION TO QUOTE FROM *An Illustrated History of Russia* RY JOEL CARMICHAEL; THE NEW YORK TIMES MAGAZINE AND HARRY SCHWARTZ FOR PERMISSION TO QUOTE FROM "MARX TO KHRUSHCHEV: A FOUR ACT DRAMA," NOVEMBER 12, 1961.

PUBLISHED SIMULTANEOUSLY IN CANADA BY LONGMANS CANADA, LIMITED, TORONTO

PRINTED IN THE UNITED STATES OF AMERICA BY GEORGE MCKIBBIN & SON, NEW YORK

To Page

The manuscript of this book was reviewed by several officials of the U. S. Department of State, where the author is now serving in the Bureau of International Organization Affairs. However, the book was in an advanced stage of preparation, and arrangement had been made for publication, before the writer joined the Department's staff. The analyses and conclusions are the responsibility of the writer alone and are not presented as official U.S. policy.

ACKNOWLEDGMENTS

A writer of this kind of book is indebted to countless other authors of books, articles, pamphlets, studies and reports; and to experiences, speeches and conversations beyond recall. But it would be negligent of the present author not to acknowledge that he is particularly beholden:

To the Council on Foreign Relations, for its thirteen volumes, *The United States in World Affairs,* which provided an invaluable chronology of post-war events;

To Edward Crankshaw, for an initial skepticism about ideology as an unmitigated blessing to the Communists;

To George Steiner's article "Homer and the Scholars," for an unexpected insight into the basic flaw in certain contemporary analyses of the Cold War;

To Theron Raines for suggesting the book in the first place;

To Michael W. Moynihan, for a critical and helpful reading of the manuscript;

To Fiona Field and Sydney Hollander, for indefatigable research assistance; and

To Tommy, Sally, Frazer, Rush, Ariel, Page and Remington, for their tolerant silence which permitted me to wrestle with this octopus in relative privacy.

T. W. W., Jr.

Washington, D.C.,
February 14, 1962

TABLE OF CONTENTS

PART ONE

THE GREAT CONFRONTATION

CHAPTER ONE

How Did We Get into This Mess?

The bloody road to Berlin lay through North Africa, Sicily, the Anzio beachhead . . . through Stalingrad, through Normandy Beach, Remagen, the Bulge, and way stations to the Wagnerian bunker in Berlin.

The price for Tokyo was paid at Guadalcanal, Saipan, and Iwo Jima . . . at Midway and the Coral Sea . . . at Hiroshima and Nagasaki before surrender on the battleship in Tokyo Bay.

On August 11, 1945, history's worst war was over.

The victories were total; the boys were coming home; arms and armies would be junked; rationing would soon be over; taxes would drop; normalcy would come back to roost in the United States; and the United Nations would keep the peace.

Or so it seemed to most of the citizens of a land which had never known national frustration except with a Great Depression, nor serious conflict with other nations except in wars—which it invariably won. So it seemed to a people who had been taught by history that they were masters of their own fate and that, by definition, the future is brighter than the past.

A decade and a half after the end of the war, six members of the United States cabinet were in Tokyo, meeting with their opposite numbers of the Japanese government. They were searching for better ways to co-ordinate their policies, better ways to channel the product of Japan's booming economy for their mutual prosperity and for co-operative development of poorer nations in Southeast Asia. If there was any rancor between former enemies, it was not evident as United States and Japanese allies worked through their peaceful agenda.

A decade and a half after the end of the war the Chancellor of the German Federal Republic was in Washington for three days of intimate talks with the President of the United States. If there were any difficulties between them, they concerned the tactics of operating their alliance or the adequacy of German efforts to ease the strain on the United States balance of payments.

But in Berlin, at about that time, American tanks were drawn up in Friederichstrasse, gun-to-gun with Russian tanks across the wall which divides that city. The victorious Allies had occupied it in 1945, and were to remain until the peace treaties could be written. Behind the wall, all of Eastern and part of Central Europe were controlled by the Soviet Union.

A decade and a half after the end of World War II, Chiang Kai-shek was holed up on an island refuge and China was in the hands of the Chinese Communists. . . . Communist and anti-Communist forces in Laos were separated only by a shaky armistice. . . . Communist guerrillas controlled much of the countryside in the free half of Viet-Nam. . . . Fidel Castro was building a totalitarian party to lead Cuba down the road to communism. . . . Algerians were rioting in Paris while Frenchmen were rioting in Algiers. . . . Russia was putting pressure on Finland while Western Allies were trying not to get pushed entirely out of West Berlin. . . . The atmosphere over Germany and Japan —and everywhere in between—was polluted with radioactive fallout from the testing of Soviet nuclear bombs, one of which was 2,500 times more powerful than the horror that fell on Hiroshima.

In the fall of 1961 President Kennedy said starkly at a press conference: "We happen to be passing through the most dangerous period in history."

This lean comment seemed to convey a sense of impending climax in what had come to be known as the cold war. It was a curious form of nonwar struggle which did not seem to yield to conventional concepts of victory.

The enemy, by public acclaim, was "communism"—but the enemy had many faces. By 1961 there were sure signs of public frustration and confusion about cold war and communism. The following fragments, for example, appeared in the public prints during a brief period in mid-1961.

According to a mass-circulation magazine:

> We must win the cold war. Our choice is implacable fight to force Communism's retreat—or face liberty's own surrender.

According to a national news magazine:

> Khrushchev, bouncier than ever, gives the impression of a man who has the world by the tail on a downhill pull. Everything seems to be going his way.

According to a prominent businessman:

> The Western allies have been so thoroughly demoralized by communist tactics of confusion . . . it is as if the West has been collaborating in the plans for its own destruction . . . the free world is being steadily and ever more rapidly cut down. . . .

According to a syndicated columnist:

> The only way to understand Khrushchev is to face up to communism itself.

According to a distinguished radio commentator:

> He [Khrushchev] has concluded that the Western Alliance cannot be pulled together, that North Africa will soon be wide open to Communist exploitation with Central Africa to follow, that Southeast Asia is rapidly crumbling into Communist hands, that our Latin American flank is being turned. He is now sure that the great game of isolating the U.S., then impoverishing it, then breaking its will, is all over save for our helpless, thrashing convulsions. . . .

According to a United States Senator:

> Someday there is either going to be world-wide communism or world-wide acceptance of the fact that man is a free child of God.

According to the governor of an eastern state:

> We've got to stand right up to Khrushchev. We've got to call a spade a spade. We can't back down.

And according to a four-star general:

> We have been on the losing end for too long a time. . . . We certainly cannot afford to lose any more areas around this world. The time has come to start winning.

Not a ray of light about the cold war in all these words; not a single clue to policy or action in any of the advice.

Yet the cold war and communism already had produced a library of literature, much of it by authors seeking the one blinding truth about communism—by rummaging in the wastebaskets of communist literature for the secret design of the master plan for communist world conquest. At the other extreme, a professor at a southern university produced a two-volume history of the cold war which went to great lengths to place the blame on an unrelieved pattern of American stupidity and error. He traced the whole business back to that nasty speech by Winston Churchill in 1946, when he mentioned the "iron curtain." All in all, the expert advice was strangely unsatisfying. Small wonder, then, that a reporter for the *Washington Post and Times-Herald,* after three weeks of traveling around the country in 1961, reported the rise of a "let's-do-something mood"—a mood that was "one almost of belligerence."

Moods can change quickly; and perhaps this one would be transitory. But at the end of 1961 two questions seemed to hang heavy in the air: How did we get into this mess? When do we start winning the cold war?

It will be many years before historians, blessed with the gift of perspective, can untangle the crazy-quilt of world affairs from the end of World War II through the first frantic year of the Kennedy Administration. Even then we may never know what motivated men—especially those for whom conspiracy is a way of life. And we may still be puzzled by many parts of the story: after all, there is no accepted explanation for the fall of Rome, and Russia was an enigma before Lenin was born.

But even now there is *some* perspective on *some* events.

At least there is a simple record of *what* happened, and in what circumstances, even if the *whys* remain a mystery. Even if the one blinding truth proves permanently illusive, even if the easy answer is hard to come by, we can still follow Al Smith's immortal prescription: "Let's look at the record."

The chapters that follow attempt to do just that, looking at the record of the cold war as a struggle between the United States and the U.S.S.R.; at "communism itself" and how the Communist world is built; then at the multiple revolutions crowding the cold war arena.

Finally, there is something of an outcry of faith based on one man's reading of the record of the cold war and the prospects for "victory."

CHAPTER TWO

Harry Truman Versus Joe Stalin

There are a number of versions as to when the cold war started, and anyone is free to pick his own date.

Some people prefer to think it began way back in Greece with the subversive idea that men had the brains to decide their own affairs in open debate, without benefit of kings or emperors.

Some date the cold war from the Bolshevik Revolution, when the first Communist Party came into power, thus acquiring an operational base for a conspiracy against all non-Communist systems everywhere.

Others date the cold war from Stalin's decision, which certainly was made by early 1945, to go it alone at the end of the war, to abandon the anti-Hitler alliance and move Soviet power into any available vacuum.

Still others prefer a later date.

Nevertheless, it has been observed incontrovertibly that it takes two make a fight. Our story of the cold war therefore begins in March of 1946, for it was then that the United States first moved to throw its power across the path of an expanding Soviet Union. As it turned out, this step ultimately led to a confrontation of the United States and Russia across frontiers extending from the Arctic tip of Norway to Japan. A strong case therefore can be made that the cold war was joined in March 1946, six months after the end of World War II in the Pacific.

The event which touched it off was President Harry

Truman's decision to stop an apparent Soviet drive to take over Iran. This was the first in a series of initiatives and counterinitiatives which characterized the beginning of the cold war; this initial phase was to last from 1946 to about 1953. The general climate of relations between the United States and the U.S.S.R. at the time is worth recalling.

American expectations of happy postwar relations with the Soviet Union, emotionally buoyed by public admiration for the exploits of the Red Army, were not easily abandoned. There was much cause for disappointment and even alarm about Soviet behavior: the Russian-manipulated installation of all Communist governments in Bulgaria and Rumania; the first pressure on Turkey to cede the provinces of Kars and Ardahan; the unilateral Soviet action in drawing the western border of Poland; the Soviet bid for Konigsberg, for a revision of the treaty governing the Dardanelles, for a share in control of the Ruhr, for a mandate over a former Italian colony in North Africa, for a bigger hand in the occupation of Japan. These and other Soviet moves led to disenchantment.

Within months after the end of the war, the Yalta agreements hammered out by Roosevelt, Churchill, and Stalin were beginning to resemble a scrap of paper. Meanwhile, a dreary series of meetings of foreign ministers to work out peace treaties were producing more in-fighting than agreement.

Some people in policy positions quickly became convinced that there was no hope of getting along peacefully with Stalin's Russia. George Kennan, then chargé d'affaires at the United States Embassy in Moscow, filed an eight-thousand word cable in which he drew deeply on Russian history to describe a nation which had "learned to seek security only in patient but deadly struggle for the total destruction of rival power, never in compacts and compromises with it." And Winston Churchill journeyed to Fulton, Missouri, to warn the world: "From Stettin in the Baltic to Trieste in the Adriatic an iron curtain has descended across the continent. . . . I do not believe that Soviet Russia desires war. What they desire is the fruits of war and the indefinite expansion of their power and doctrines."

Yet the picture did not seem totally black. After all, the Soviet Union had joined the United Nations. At the mid-1945 Potsdam Conference agreements had been reached for treating Germany as a single economic unit and for a reasonable approach to reparations from Germany. An armistice was reached in the Greek civil war in January 1946, with the provision that a plebiscite be held on the return of the king and a national election, under Allied supervision. General George Marshall had negotiated a cease-fire agreement between Chiang Kai-shek and the Chinese Communists. Stalin had accepted the proposal for a United Nations Atomic Energy Commission. In general, there were islands of agreement within seas of disagreement in the course of the meetings of the foreign ministers. Also, there was an inclination among some American officials, including Secretary of State James F. Byrnes, to believe that the problem was simply one of negotiating out the legal clauses of peace treaties to bring the war to a formal close. Some even believed that the real antagonists were Russia and Britain, and that the proper role of the United States was to help compromise their conflicting foreign policy interests.

Besides, there seemed to be explanations, or at least excuses, for the exasperating behavior of the Russians immediately after the war. Soviet occupation forces in the middle of Europe had supply lines running through the Balkans, so Russia naturally would want to make sure of a friendly attitude on the part of nations astride those lines. It was pointed out that Stalin would be concerned with the security of his western frontier, and that he would be fearful of a renascent and aggressive Germany. Stalin's behavior in Eastern Europe seemed to some all more justified when it became known that Churchill and Anthony Eden had agreed with Stalin in 1944 to give the U.S.S.R. a free hand in Bulgaria and Rumania in return for allowing Britain a free hand in Greece.

Anyhow, didn't the United States have a world monopoly on the atomic bomb? In any event, United States public opinion was not prepared to give up easily its serene vision of the postwar world. President Truman was spanked smartly by editorial writers just for sitting on the same platform with Churchill when he delivered his iron curtain speech—which was generally regarded in the United States press as unnecessarily provocative, if not downright belligerent.

So in early 1946 there was a bit of alarm and some disappointment, but hope still prevailed for a "return to normalcy" in the postwar world. And the general public would much rather read about Jackie Robinson at Ebbets Field than Comrade Vishinsky at Bucharest.

But to President Truman the situation in Iran in March 1946 looked like an open-and-shut case. The background was less complicated than the situation in Eastern Europe: Russia had occupied northern Iran while the British and Americans had occupied southern Iran to open a back-door supply line to the Red Army. At the Teheran Conference in 1943 it had been agreed that all would withdraw within six months after the armistice in Europe. The United

States and the British withdrew before the deadline of March 6, 1946, but the Russians did not. Instead, the Iranian Tudeh party set up an independent republic of Azerbaijan in northern Iran under a Communist named Jaafar Pishevari, who had done the same thing under the protection of Russian troops in the 1920s. A Soviet propaganda campaign was launched against the Iranian government, and when Iranian troops moved toward the northern part of their country, they were blocked by Soviet tanks.

All this had not passed without protest. Complaints were made by Iran directly to the Soviet Union—without satisfaction. The Americans and British supported Iran with diplomatic notes to Moscow—without result. The case was appealed to the Security Council of the United Nations—to no avail. Secretary of State James F. Byrnes made a tough speech in which he said, "We will not and we cannot stand aloof if force or the threat of force is used contrary to purposes and principles of the Charter," but Stalin did not seem to be listening.

Then, during the first week in March, a Soviet column started moving south from Azerbaijan toward the capital of Teheran, and another swung west toward the Turkish and Iraqi frontiers. An American military attaché reported seeing a Russian tank within twenty-five miles of the capital.

It was at this point that President Truman decided to act. Consulting only Secretary of State Byrnes, Mr. Truman sent a message to Generalissimo Stalin—the exact text of which is still a state secret. Recounting the incident in his memoirs, Mr. Truman said that he was concerned at the prospect of a Russian pincer on the eastern flank of Turkey, but even more alarmed by Russia's "callous disregard of the rights of a small nation and her own solemn promises." He felt it was clear that "Russia was determined to have her own way and to ignore the United States and the U.N. alike."

On the day following Mr. Truman's decision, the newspapers reported what seemed to be a routine protest to Moscow about the continued presence of Russian troops in Iran. It was not the first. But thirteen years later, during a series of lectures to students at Columbia University, citizen Truman described the message as an "ultimatum" in which he threatened to deploy United States naval and ground forces in the Persian Gulf—an area, incidentally, whose history and geography were thoroughly familiar to the American President. The firmness of the message to Stalin is confirmed by the urgency with which Mr. Truman at that time persuaded Averell Harriman to take the post of Ambassador to London. The President told Harriman that he was in "serious trouble with the Russians," and that while he thought Stalin would back down in Iran, he could not be sure; his ultimatum conceivably could lead to war, and it was most important for the Americans and the British to be in agreement on every step.

But this time Stalin was listening. There was a quick shifting of Soviet gears. The Russian Ambassador in Teheran reopened negotiations with the Iranian government in a much friendlier mood. At the United Nations, Andrei Gromyko tried desperately but unsuccessfully to postpone a new Security Council hearing on the Iranian complaint, which was scheduled for March 25. On March 26 he announced that Soviet troops would be withdrawn from Iran within five or six weeks "unless unforeseen circumstances arise." On April 25 the Soviets announced they would pull out the Red Army within a month—which they subsequently did.

Though hardly anyone knew it at the time, a secret

ultimatum from President Truman to Generalissimo Stalin liberated Iran from Soviet occupation, turned back a Russian flanking movement against Turkey and Iraq, and won the Security Council some credit for putting out a fire. Harry Truman scratched a line across the border of northern Iran and warned Stalin to stay out. What no one knew at the time, including Truman or Stalin, was that the United States had made the first of a series of countermoves in the yet-undeclared cold war which would dominate world affairs for at least fifteen years, and probably much longer. Truman's note to Stalin was the first United States move under what would later be termed the doctrine of containment.

Perhaps when Stalin pulled his troops out of Iran and removed that item from the agenda of the Security Council, he expected to get control by less drastic means. For a while it looked as though he might.

During this crisis the Iranian government fell. A bitterly anti-Communist premier was replaced by Ahmed Ghavam-es-Saltaneh, who was considered to be much more amenable to compromise with the Soviet Union and its puppet Tudeh party. Within a few months after the Russians withdrew their troops, Ghavam appointed one of Pishevari's men as governor general of Azerbaijan, opened the door for a much stronger delegation from Azerbaijan in the Parliament, and took three Tudeh members into his cabinet—one as vice-premier. The odds against Iran were lengthening again.

But then the Communists made a mistake to which they are abnormally prone: they overplayed their hand. A Tudeh party leader called a strike in Abadan and other oil centers in the southern part of the country, and it led to riots, damage, and death. That brought British troops to the Iraqi-Iranian border. More important, it touched off a revolt of several tribes in southern Iran, with the leaders demanding that the Tudeh party members be thrown out of the cabinet and that the southern provinces receive greater voting weight in the Parliament to offset the increased representation proposed for Azerbaijan.

The besieged Premier Ghavam proceeded to play one pressure group off against the other. He negotiated with the southern rebels, accepted most of their demands, arrested some Tudeh agents in Teheran, dropped the Tudeh cabinet members, and ordered the army to supervise the election in Azerbaijan. Pishevari called for armed resistance, but when the troops arrived in Tabriz, there was none. The Tudeh regime collapsed. Pishevari escaped back to the Soviet Union, and when the election was over, the Communists held only two seats in the Parliament.

The full story of Ghavam's elaborate maneuvering—and the role of British and American diplomacy—may not come to light for a long time. But when it does, someone may name an anti-Communist society in his honor.

In the meantime it had become all too clear by the late spring of 1946 that the Russians were not going to live up to the Potsdam commitment to treat Germany as an economic unit. The United States reluctantly started to consolidate the non-Soviet zones, thus tacitly admitting the indefinite division of Germany.

Then, in the summer of 1946, the Soviets proposed to Turkey, Britain, and the United States an end to international supervision of the Dardanelles, control of the straits by Russia and Turkey alone, and the establishment of Soviet air and naval bases on Turkish territory. This was accompanied by a Communist propaganda onslaught against the "Nazis" and "imperialists" in Ankara—keyed to agitation for an independent Armenia and renewed claims not only for the Turkish provinces of Kars and Ardahan, but for Artvin and other Turkish districts as well. To back up the diplomatic notes and the propaganda, twenty-five divisions of the Red Army maneuvered along the southern border of the Caucasus.

This time President Truman asked the advice of the State, War, and Navy departments and the Joint Chiefs of Staff. They concurred in a decision to back up Turkey. President Truman is reported to have concluded the decisive meeting of his advisers with this comment: "We might as well find out now, rather than five or ten years from now, whether the Russians are determined to take over the world."

What he found out was this: after two rounds of diplomatic exchanges in which the United States and Britain strongly backed an adamant Turkey, and while units of the United States fleet headed by the aircraft carrier *Franklin D. Roosevelt* paid "courtesy calls" in the Mediterranean, Stalin decided to stay his hand in Turkey.

But only to tighten the screws on Greece. The various techniques of Soviet pressure were well co-ordinated. Communist propaganda switched from the Turkish "nazis" and "imperialists" to the Greek "monarcho-fascists"; at the United Nations the delegate from the Ukraine accused the Greeks of persecuting minorities with British help and with plotting to grab part of Albania. At the Peace Conference in Paris the Bulgarians put in a bid for a piece of Thrace, the Yugoslavs argued for an independent Macedonia, and Mr. Molotov charged Greece with terror and repression at home and with plans for aggression abroad. Simultaneously, the once-disarmed bands of Greek guerrillas under the Communist-led ELAS again turned up in the north of Greece, freshly trained and equipped. The Greek government claimed they had been sheltered, trained, supplied, and provided with border protection by Yugoslavia, Bulgaria, and Albania—a claim which later was confirmed by a United Nations Commission of Investigation.

Through the fall and early winter of 1946 affairs in Greece went from bad to worse. The Greek army was in no shape physically or psychologically to put up much of a fight. Communications were broken and government control receded to a shrunken area around the capital. Refugees from burned-out villages shuffled into Athens. Foreign exchange was exhausted, the prospective budgetary deficit was three times the money in circulation, prices went wild, and a deep sense of panic infected the country.

In response to Greek soundings for financial help, the United States in January sent an economic mission to investigate. By the latter part of February, the mission cabled its views. There was no pussy-footing in the conclusion: either the United States would come through at once with large-scale assistance over a period of years to be handled by United States administrators and technicians on the spot, or the Greeks would soon join the roster of peoples who live behind the iron curtain. That was the gist of it.

A few days after this report reached Washington the prime minister and foreign minister of Greece sent another urgent, formal appeal for financial and military help and for "experienced American . . . personnel" to run an aid program and "train the young people of Greece to assume their responsibilities. . . ."

Between these two messages something else happened which put the case of aid to Greece on an urgent yes-or-no basis.

Late in the afternoon of February 21, the First Secretary

of the British Embassy called on the Department of State to deliver a pair of notes. The subjects were Greece and Turkey. Each note included some background formalities recalling previous understandings between Britain and the United States about the strategic importance of Greece and Turkey and previous agreements that Britain should carry the main load in these countries. Each note included some financial projections on the extent of the help that was now needed, as well as an estimate of the current situation. Briefly, the notes warned that Greece was on the point of collapse and that Turkey could either support its economy or its army, but not both.

Then came the climax: His Majesty's government had decided reluctantly that it could no longer afford to provide support for Greece and Turkey. It would be obliged to stop financial and military assistance to Greece on March 30, and it hoped the United States would pick up the job as of that date. This lit the fuse that exploded three weeks later into the Truman Doctrine—and less than four months later, into the Marshall Plan.

A careful chronicle of the "major turning point in American history" that took place between the delivery of the British notes on February 21 and the passage of the Marshall Plan on June 5 has been recorded by Joseph M. Jones in *The Fifteen Weeks.* Mr. Jones was in the middle of these events, and found them a "spectacle of the United States government operating at its very finest, efficiently and effectively, and of the American people responding to leadership in a manner equally splendid." And he sets the high lights against the background of a "much wider situation" in which they took place.

For Turkey and Greece—and the continuing crisis in

Iran—were not the only trouble spots during the year that elapsed between Truman's ultimatum to Stalin and the delivery of the British notes to the State Department.

In the fall of 1946 open guerrilla warfare broke out in Indo-China, harbinger of a Communist decision to go on the offensive through South and Southeast Asia.

In January 1947, General Marshall gave up his hopeless mission to negotiate peace between Chiang Kai-shek and Mao Tse-tung and returned to replace James Byrnes as Secretary of State.

In February the Communists in Poland, by terror, falsification, arrest, manipulation—and with the Red Army standing by—rigged an election that spelled the end of freedom for that country and the end of the Yalta agreement as well.

And in Europe the Communist parties were doing their best to parlay postwar exhaustion and wreckage into chaos. In September 1946 the United States announced that it would keep armed forces in Europe as long as they were needed. But worst of all, the stark fact was that Britain was broke.

Nevertheless, there was little evidence that the American people were ready for the shock of the Truman Doctrine. There had been some public anger about Soviet doings in Poland and elsewhere, but most people still seemed to hope that the United Nations would solve our problems. Henry Wallace was still in the cabinet preaching eternal friendship between the United States and the U.S.S.R.

And in November 1946 the voters returned a Republican majority to the Senate and the House of Representatives, an assembly which was acclaimed promptly and widely as "Taft's Congress." Representative Taber, new chairman of the House Appropriations Committee, announced that he would "take the meat axe to government frills." And as for foreign affairs, Senator Taft announced: ". . . it would be ironical if this Congress which really has its heart set on straightening out our domestic affairs would end up in being besieged by foreign problems."

Perhaps the mood, and the hopes, of the country concerning "foreign problems" were best illustrated by the Acheson-Lilienthal plan for control of the atom, which was presented to the United Nations by Bernard Baruch in June 1946. This offer, which might have gone down as one of the greatest single acts of history, proposed that the United Nations take full control of the American monopoly on atomic weaponry, research, facilities, and knowledge; and that it supervise, under international control, the management of every element of atomic industry, down to and including the mining of uranium. The proposal may not have been perfect and might well have been altered in various respects. But the Soviets immediately denounced it as propaganda, proposed a thoroughly unacceptable substitute, and launched a game of evasion and deception that culminated fifteen years later with the detonation of a fifty-megaton terror bomb on October 30, 1961.

Yet six months after the Acheson-Lilienthal plan was presented to the United Nations, *Time* magazine was chiding old friend Bernard Baruch for "inflexible diplomacy." In its December 30, 1946, issue, *Time* said that Baruch's attitude toward Soviet proposals "gave the Russians, at least, some slight ground for yelling atomic blackmail." And after reporting a Baruch concession at a meeting of the U.N.'s Atomic Energy Commission, the editors concluded with one of their less prophetic thoughts: ". . . now that Baruch had come down off his mountain, maybe Gromyko would come down off his."

A few years later, such tolerance of Soviet behavior

could not be expected outside the pages of the *Daily Worker*. But *Time* seemed to reflect the general temper of the country when the British delivered their historic notes about Greece and Turkey. The ultimatum to Stalin in the Iranian affair was still Mr. Truman's secret. The showdown with Russia over the Dardanelles had been handled through diplomatic channels, plus some "courtesy calls" by the Navy which the President himself could order. But the case of Greece and Turkey in the spring of 1947 was different. The public would have to be consulted, and the Congress not only would have to agree to a policy, but to appropriate taxpayers' funds for use in distant countries at a time of peace.

Yet within six days after the delivery of the British notes—six days which included a weekend—the State, War, and Navy Departments and the Joint Chiefs of Staff had reached an agreed position; the cabinet had been consulted; estimates of Greek and Turkish needs had been prepared; aid programs had been drawn up; messages had been drafted; and President Truman was ready to discuss with Congressional leaders what he called "the most terrible decision a President has ever had to make."

After Mr. Truman and members of his cabinet briefed Congressional leaders at a special meeting in the White House in the second week of March, Senator Arthur Vandenberg, the isolationist-turned-internationalist, paused on his way out by the Presidential desk of his old Senate colleague.

"Mr. President," said Vandenberg, "if that's what you want, there's only one way to put it over. You must make a personal appearance before the Congress and scare hell out of the country."

A few days later, on March 12, 1947, President Truman did just that. Standing in a deadly serious mood before a joint session of the Senate and the House of Representatives, he said:

> The very existence of the Greek state is today threatened by the terrorist activities of several thousand armed men, led by Communists. . . . The Greek government is unable to cope with the situation.
>
> Greece must have assistance if it is to become a self-supporting and self-respecting democracy.
>
> The United States must supply that assistance. . . . There is no other country to which democratic Greece can turn. . . .
>
> The future of Turkey as an independent and economically sound state is clearly of no less importance. . . .
>
> As in the case of Greece, if Turkey is to have the assistance it needs, the United States must supply it. . . .
>
> I am fully aware of the broad implications involved. . . . We shall not realize our objectives, however, unless we are willing to help free peoples to maintain their free institutions and their national integrity against aggressive movements that seek to impose upon them totalitarian regimes. . . .
>
> We must take immediate and resolute action. . . .
>
> This is a serious course upon which we embark.
>
> I would not recommend it except that the alternative is much more serious. . . .

President Truman's address triggered an alarm that was hard to ignore. The tough, simple, unqualified language served to narrow the proposal to a take-it-or-leave-it basis. Either the United States was going to "help free peoples to maintain their free institutions and their national integrity against aggressive movements," or it was not. There was little or no room for desultory talk about details, for suggesting that we wait a bit longer and see what happens, or for quibbling about the size of the program or the amount of money needed to back it.

There was opposition, in and out of Congress, from both ends of the political spectrum and from those who still held that peace could be won by being nice to the Russians. But as the Administration spelled out its case in Congress, with Senator Vandenberg handling parliamentary strategy, a bipartisan majority was coming to the grim agreement that United States intervention in Greece and Turkey was the best of a bad bargain.

Most of the press and the radio commentators rallied around to the same conclusion. Within a week or so it was also clear that public opinion had been shocked into going along. The foreign relations committees in Congress first authorized the plunge into Greece and Turkey. On April 22 the Senate voted the appropriations to carry it out by nearly three to one; and on May 8 the House approved by better than two and a half to one. Ships had been loaded with supplies for Greece and Turkey before the last vote was taken.

Thus Turkey acquired the means to support its economy and to keep a big army as well. Thus Greece received, on a crash basis, the financial help, the military hardware, and the administrative know-how to turn the tables on the Communist guerrillas and eventually to restore order and recovery in the country. Thus, within a few weeks in the spring of 1947, the United States, after Congressional debate and by Act of Congress, turned its historic foreign policy upside down and ventured out to meet the world—moving to counter a threat to peace before it had been attacked directly.

And thus the line that Truman scratched along the border of northern Iran in 1946, the line that Stalin had been warned not to cross, was extended in 1947 around the borders of Turkey and Greece. The great confrontation was shaping up. The cold war had not yet been baptized. But it was out in the open.

The Other Half of the Walnut

Just five days after the United States Senate voted appropriations for aid to Greece and Turkey, a meeting of the foreign ministers of the wartime Allies broke up in Moscow after weeks of fruitless haggling over the administration of Germany, the frontier with Poland, reparations payments, and other issues which were stuck as firmly at the end of the meeting as they were at the beginning. It was George Marshall's first international conference as Secretary of State, and he left Moscow convinced that little could be expected from further negotiations with Stalin's Russia. On the way out of the Soviet Union, the American delegation flew over a Europe which was to be described by Winston Churchill a few weeks later in these words: "What is Europe now? It is a rubble-heap, a charnel house, a breeding ground of pestilence and hate."

Behind that burst of Churchillian rhetoric were cold statistics of low food production and crop failures; of lagging coal output and bad winters; of disappointing industrial production and disrupted transport; of trade patterns snarled by war shortages. Above all, national treasuries were running out of the foreign exchange which alone could purchase from America the things which were needed for recovery. Unemployment was high. Hunger was spreading. Black markets were rampant. Tuberculosis was increasing. Europe and the Europeans were wounded and sick, and hope was hard to sustain.

During the return flight from Moscow of the United States mission to the Foreign Ministers' Conference, General Marshall directed his staff to start work immediately on a major American initiative to help put Europe back on its feet and thus buttress the Western world against a Soviet Union which seemed set on the promotion of "pestilence and hate." This is where the Marshall Plan was conceived, high over the Atlantic, in response to Stalin's adamant bargaining over Germany. As President Truman later said, the Marshall Plan was related to the Truman Doctrine like "the other half of the walnut."

The "near miracle" of the Marshall Plan is too well known to need anything but the most passing reference here. General Marshall suggested, during a commencement address at Harvard in June 1947, that the United States would consider co-operating with a major European recovery effort. His initiative was seized "with both hands" by Britain's Foreign Minister Ernest Bevin, and the nations of Western Europe drew up plans under forced draft during the sweltering summer that followed. After American revision the program was put to the Congress, which—again guided and prodded by

Senator Vandenberg—approved and voted the appropriations. The Europeans set up an organization to reconcile national plans and divide the aid. Paul Hoffman threw his sales and executive talents into the crash organization of a new government agency to run the program from Washington. Averell Harriman left his post as Secretary of Commerce and headed for Paris to establish headquarters for some sixteen missions of Americans hastily-recruited but dominated with a sense of excitement and mission. United States supplies began moving eastward across the Atlantic, and the country's prestige was never higher.

No one can say for sure that without the Marshall Plan all of Europe would have fallen to the Communists, but no one can deny it with any assurance either.

In the end, a job which was to have taken four years at a cost of $17,000,000,000 was completed in less than three years at a cost of $12,500,000,000. More than that, Europe had learned the "habit of co-operation," and a chain of events was set in motion which finally led not only to recovery but also to the economic renaissance of Europe, and to the revival of the European dream of unification which had stirred philosophers and statesmen for centuries. All this is a well-known piece of contemporary history.

But one passage from the now-historic Marshall speech at Harvard cannot be quoted too often: "Our policy is directed not against any party or doctrine but against hunger, poverty, desperation and chaos." This was to say, among other things, that the offer was open to Eastern Europe and to the Soviet Union itself. In fact, Mr. Bevin and French Foreign Minister Bidault immediately invited the Russians to join them in accepting General Marshall's initiative. But there is no room in communist dogma for constructive con between capitalist nations; there was no room in plans for collaboration with the West; and there was n in the Soviet Union or Eastern Europe for joint operations with United States aid missions. Despite Russia's desperate needs, the whole thing was too much for the Soviet leaders to swallow.

After trying to persuade the British and French that the Marshall Plan was a plot to short-circuit an American post-war depression by invading the markets of Europe, Mr. Molotov withdrew from a preparatory meeting in Paris. The Russians forced Czechoslovakia and Poland to withdraw their initial decisions to join the recovery program. So much stemmed from this Russian decision that the distinguished British scholar Edward Crankshaw prefers to consider it the starting date of the cold war.

From that point on the Communists worked desperately to defeat the Marshall Plan, and did much to insure its success.

The first step was to try to stop it before it could begin. Strikes were called throughout Europe in the hope of wrecking the economy beyond repair before help began to arrive. These reached their climax in the sabotage-by-flooding of coal mines in northern France by the Communist-led miners' union. But the strikes fell far short of their goal. More than that, they helped to turn the rank and file against Communist leadership, and helped inspire the organization of anti-Communist unions. Thus Communist violence backfired. Eventually it led to a split in the Communist-dominated World Federation of Trade Unions, and the later growth of the present International Confederation of Free Trade Unions—no small asset to the non-Communist world in succeeding years.

Meanwhile, the Communists made a major effort to take

Italy out of the picture. While the Marshall Plan was still under discussion in the United States, massive Soviet support was poured into the Italian Communist party in the hope of a victory in the national elections which were to be held in the spring of 1948. A Communist success was predicted generally by Western correspondents in Rome. But with the help of an Interim Aid Bill for Italy and Austria, passed by a special session of the Congress in the autumn of 1947; with a large-scale letter-writing campaign by Americans of Italian origin; and with the chances good for ultimate passage of the Marshall Plan, the Italian voters defeated what turned out to be the last chance of a Communist victory in a free election in Western Europe.

No one can say for sure just how much the Russians themselves helped secure the passage of the Marshall Plan legislation. But it is just possible that Western Europe owes its good health, and perhaps its freedom, to Stalin's decision to grab Czechoslovakia at exactly the time he chose to do it.

The techniques of Communist take-over in Eastern and Central Europe will be touched upon in a subsequent chapter. It is enough to mention here that the Communists could have captured Czechoslovakia at any time after it was overrun by the Soviet Army in 1945. Czechoslovakia was surrounded on three sides by Soviet-controlled states. The Red Army was within easy call. Democratic Czech leaders were paralyzed by fear of a vengeful Germany and obsessed with the need to maintain Soviet friendship. The final coup was precipitated by a cabinet crisis in which the Social Democrats opened the way for the Communists to apply the last turn of the screw against President Edward Benes, who capitulated in the establishment of a garden-variety Communist dictatorship.

A few weeks later Jan Masaryk—the former foreign

minister, son of the first president of Czechoslovakia, and well-known friend of the West—was found dead in a courtyard. Whether he jumped or was murdered may never be known. But his broken body symbolized to the rest of the world what had happened to his country, and if his death was a willful act it may have been the most useful suicide in history. As far as the United States Congress was concerned, this act was decisive. There was no further doubt about the fate of the Marshall Plan legislation. The brutality of the seizure of Czechoslovakia had the effect of an ice-cold shower for many people in Western Europe and the United States. Those who had longed for good relations with Russia, those who had tried so hard to explain or excuse Soviet behavior, had little more to say. One week after Masaryk's body was picked up from the courtyard in Prague, Britain, France, Belgium, Holland, and Luxembourg signed the military alliance called Western Union which was to serve as the European nucleus for NATO.

Meanwhile, in reaction to the establishment of the Organization for European Economic Cooperation to administer the recovery of Europe, the Soviet Union set up the Council of Economic Mutual Aid. Ostensibly its purpose was to coordinate economic development in Eastern Europe, but actually it was meant to gear the satellite economies to the needs of the U.S.S.R. In addition the Russians revived the Comintern, the Communist international which had been disbanded in deference to the sensibilities of Russia's wartime allies. Only now it was called the Cominform. A priority task was to sabotage the Marshall Plan.

As ships began to arrive in Europe with American supplies, Communist-led dockers' unions refused to unload them and tried to paralyze European ports. Their cause was less than popular with governments or the general public. Troops unloaded ships and the strikes collapsed.

But for another three years the Communists mounted the most massive and best-financed propaganda campaign ever witnessed to convince Europeans that the Marshall Plan was a prescription for slavery in the service of Wall Street monopoly capitalists. Every medium of propaganda which the Communists controlled or could buy was used to the hilt. Communist posters plastered the walls of the cities. Handbills were passed out to the workers leaving their factories. News sheets appeared on the walls of remote villages. Counter-propaganda was torn down or painted red by Communist crews in the streets by night. The radio programs from Eastern Europe kept up a drumfire of anti-Marshall Plan messages.

Every pretext was seized for a protest meeting, a rally, a speech, a demonstration. Every conceivable form of front organization was established to lend respectability. And if respectability didn't work, there were other techniques. Rocks were thrown through the screens of motion-picture theaters showing newsreels of Marshall Plan projects. Riots were staged at United States information exhibits. Bundles of United States-sponsored newspapers were thrown into rivers from trains crossing bridges at night.

It was estimated that during the first several years of the European Recovery Program, the Communists spent seven times as much for propaganda as the United States spent for the Marshall Plan information service. Against these odds, the United States services worked overtime and well. The best film crews that could be assembled turned out news clips, film magazines, and documentaries at prodigious rates, and showed them not only in theaters but also in village squares where motion pictures had never been seen before. Mobile exhibits toured the roads, the rails, and the canals of Europe. Magazines, pamphlets, newspapers, press and photo services carried the news of American aid, European recovery, and the strange new story of co-operation among nations. Radio programs hit the national networks, and were beamed in from Luxembourg and Andorra for good measure.

By and large, the European governments did their best to co-operate with the American services and supplement them with their own. Europeans supplied much of the talent: at one time the United States studio in Paris in which exhibits were being built included draftsmen, designers, artists, technicians, and managers from nineteen nations, and eleven languages were needed to converse with them all. To those who were there, it was exciting business.

For several years the propaganda battle over the Marshall Plan continued. The American propagandists had much to learn at first, and they made some mistakes. But the Communists never really had a chance. Neither before nor since has Communist propaganda seriously damaged a solid institution with a progressive program. In the end, the extreme Communist effort to wreck the Marshall Plan probably was a major factor in the disillusionment that weakened Communist influence in Europe from that time forward.

Lemay's Coal and Feed Company

While the European Recovery Program was just getting under way, however, there was another major round in the cold war: the prodigious Berlin airlift.

In February 1948 the Americans, British, and French began discussing the political unification of the Western zones of Germany. Then in late March 1948 the commander of the Russian Zone of Berlin, Marshal Sokolovsky, walked out of a Control Council meeting with the startling words: "The Control Council no longer exists as an organ of government."

Only a month later the Russians started interfering with international train services out of Berlin.

On June 20 the Western occupying powers introduced a much-needed currency reform in Western Germany and Berlin, which was opposed by the Soviet Union.

On June 24 the Russians announced that since the railroads needed repairs and the road conditions along the highways were unsafe, rail and road traffic between Berlin and Western Germany would be suspended.

By July 1, traffic was at a standstill. The first major "Berlin crisis" was at hand. The Western choice was to get out of Berlin or risk war. After worried consultation, the decision was made to run the risk, and to minimize it by the drastic device of supplying Berlin entirely by air from inside West Germany, the border of which was a hundred and ten miles away. According to President Truman, it was such a stupendous undertaking that "even the Air Force chiefs themselves had serious doubts that it could be done."

But done it was. General Curtis LeMay had about a hundred and ten transports under his command in Germany, mostly two-engined C-47s. But within days four-engined C-54s were flying in from Texas, Panama, and Alaska—and what became known as the LeMay Coal and Feed Company was tackling "the trickiest traffic problem that aviation has yet produced." Flying in corridors only twenty miles wide, at staggered altitudes, in all weather, twenty-four hours a day, sometimes harrassed by Soviet fighter planes, and landing at airports only four minutes away from each other, the airlift moved an average of 1,000 metric tons of food daily in the first month of operations. By September the average was 4,000 tons, most of it coal. By the next spring the daily average was 8,000 tons. At its peak, an incredible 1,398 trips brought 13,000 tons of supplies into Berlin within a twenty-four hour period. That was the day when planes touched down at the Templehof airdrome in the middle of Berlin at a rate of one every thirty seconds.

By this time nearly a hundred Allied airmen had been killed. But Berlin had enough supplies to carry it through the next winter, and Stalin had had enough.

In late January, in answering questions put to him by Kingsbury Smith of International News Service, Stalin intimated that if the Western powers would postpone their plans for integrating their zones in Western Germany and discuss the whole matter at a meeting of the foreign ministers, the Berlin blockade might be lifted. This was checked out with the Soviet Delegate to the United Nations, Jacob Malik. It was a month before Malik got an answer from Moscow, and that needed clarification. Then Tass, in effect, confirmed the story, and the State Department announced on April 26 that "the way appears clear for a lifting of the blockade and a meeting of the Council of Foreign Ministers."

More than ten months after it began, and more than 250,000 flights later, the Berlin airlift came to an end on May 11. At midnight on May 11–May 12, Allied trains and trucks crossed the borders en route to Berlin without incident. The Western Allies were still in Berlin. The cold war was still cold. At any time the Russians could have raised the risk of war: they could have cut the Berlin water supply, which originates in the Soviet Zone.

Soviet pressure against Berlin, on top of everything else, goaded the reluctant Western democracies to reverse the course of postwar disarmament and look to their mutual defense. In April 1949, with the Berlin airlift roaring into its tenth month, the North Atlantic Treaty Organization was established at American initiative. It brought together the United States, Canada, Britain, and the nations of Western Europe—the greatest potential aggregation of military power, industrial strength, and trained manpower ever linked in common enterprise in time of peace.

The aim of NATO was the defense of the North Atlantic area, more specifically Western Europe. Its program at first was cautious: regular consultation between military staffs and an agreed but modest increase in combined armed strength. Within a little more than a year, however, two things happened which were to turn the cold war into what looked more and more like an all-out arms race.

The first of these events, in the fall of 1949, was the successful test of an atomic explosion by the Soviet Union. Everyone assumed that the Russians were working on atomic fission and everyone also assumed that sooner or later they would succeed. But the first mushroom cloud rose over the Soviet Union at least five years ahead of the earliest date predicted by Western scientists.

If this was a shock, there was a rougher one coming in less than a year. On a Sunday morning late in June 1950 the Russian-trained-and-equipped army of North Korea drove across the 38th parallel, which divided the Soviet and American occupation zones, established at the end of the war.

Three years and thirty-two days later—including more than two years of almost unbearably frustrating negotiations—the agreement was reached on an armistice line which mainly ran a few miles north of the same 38th parallel. In the interim the ill-trained American occupation troops were all but thrown off the southern tip of the peninsula before they began a brilliant comeback, which carried them well into North Korea until Communist China intervened massively. The United Nations rallied troops from fifteen nations to serve under the flag of a world community led by General Douglas MacArthur of the United States who was later dismissed from his command for wanting to carry the war into Mainland China. The cost to the United States was some 23,000 killed, 106,000 wounded, and $18,000,000,000; the cost to other U.N. forces was about 14,000 casualties. The cost to the Republic of Korea was about 300,000 military and perhaps 1,000,000 civilian casualties, 2,500,000 refugees, 600,000 houses destroyed, and damages estimated at anywhere between $1,000,000,000 and $4,000,000,000. The enemy suffered 1,500,000 to 2,000,000 military and perhaps 3,000,000 civilian casualties, and lost about 1,500 square miles of territory.

Because the Korean War was preceded by American ambivalence about its Pacific defense perimeter, because General MacArthur was removed from his command, and especially because this conflict was made the subject of bitter partisanship in the 1952 election campaign, details of the Korean story are still colored by emotion.

But when time draws the fever of domestic politics from the history of the Korean War, the skeletal facts will remain: when the Russians—contained from Norway to Iran—turned to the east and tried aggression by proxy, the United States elected to fight, eventually threw the aggressor back to where he started, and refused to be drawn into a war on the mainland of China.

Perhaps some future historian will make something of

the fact that during the Korean War President Truman made two big decisions based on two simple propositions. The first decision was to fight, and the proposition was that aggression is aggression, and must be resisted regardless of whether the aggressor is big or small or whether the action takes place in a strategically central area or in a remote one. Not all his allies nor all his advisers agreed with this proposition. The second decision was to fire General MacArthur. The proposition was that issues of peace and war are not decided by generals in the field, even hero generals, but by the Commander in Chief in Washington. Not all of President Trumans' advisers agreed with this proposition, either.

In any event, the arms race that emerged from the end of the American monopoly on atomic power and the Korean invasion combined to give the cold war a military aspect that would remain for years to come. The United States moved to a stage of semimobilization, with the defense budget shooting from $18,000,000,000 to $35,000,000,000, and NATO raised its rearmament sights and converted its consultative machinery to a permanent staff organization. America became the military partner and arms supplier of every nation that could be brought into a mutual defense arrangement. We began to thank our stars for the Marshall Plan—not so much because it helped the Europeans to rise out of misery and chaos, but because it gave them an economic base for a rearmament program which otherwise would have been impossible.

Before long the United States was to be allied with forty-two nations in military pacts around the world—NATO in Europe, SEATO in Southeast Asia, ANZUS in the South Pacific, CENTO along the upper "tier" of the Middle East, and the Rio Pact in the Western Hemisphere, along with bilateral agreements with Japan, the Philippines, Taiwan, and South Korea. Treaties were negotiated establishing American air bases in a ring around the Soviet Union. Arms flowed to the French in their foredoomed effort to restore colonial control in Indo-China. They were sent to the Philippines to help stamp out the Communist-inspired Huk rebellion. Chiang Kai-shek, in refuge on Formosa, received United States military aid, as did the Iranians—in fact, almost anyone, it seemed, who said he was prepared to fight if attacked by the Communists. By the end of the Truman Administration the doctrine of containment was nearing its logical conclusion.

Well before this, however, a large straw appeared in the wind to indicate a basic change in Soviet policy. On June 23, 1951, on the eve of the first anniversary of the Korean invasion, Jacob Malik, head of the Soviet delegation to the United Nations, the same man who confirmed Stalin's readiness to call off the Berlin blockade, was interviewed on a weekly radio program sponsored by the world organization. After a standard rehashing of Soviet complaints about the aggressive policies of the West, Mr. Malik quite unexpectedly commented that despite all this, the Korean War could be brought to a close if the belligerents really wanted to do so. He then suggested that discussions begin for a cease-fire and armistice at the 38th parallel. That started the negotiations which led ultimately to the armistice in Korea.

A year after the armistice in Korea left that country split near the 38th parallel, the Geneva conference, after months of preliminaries and eighty-seven days of negotiation, with the United States sitting dourly on the side lines, brought an end to the seven-year war in Indo-China by splitting Viet-Nam along the 17th parallel. For the first time in over twenty years, there was no formal war anywhere in the world. The peace would not last long.

It now seems likely that by mid-1951 Stalin decided that there was more to lose than to gain in further fighting in Korea. He had used the Red Army to expand the area of Soviet control. This induced the doctrine of containment. Then Stalin tested the United States will to fight at the point where military resistance seemed least likely. The United States fought back. Thus the doctrine of containment brought an end to Soviet expansion by force.

This was the first stage of cold war. It was a period in which Joe Stalin inevitably had the initiative at all points simply because the United States, by nature and by choice, cannot take the initiative in a military struggle. But Harry Truman, not so inevitably, responded to every major Soviet initiative—in Iran, in Turkey, in Greece, in Berlin, and in Korea. After seven years, the result was a stalemate.

Thus it was that during the first stage of the cold war the Soviet Union expanded the area under its control by installing Communist governments in Bulgaria, Rumania, Hungary, Poland, and Czechoslovakia—bringing approximately 59,-163,000 people and 340,453 square miles of territory within its orbit.

It also was during this period that China came under Communist control, under conditions which will be discussed in Chapter Five.

And the United States monopoly on atomic weapons became a thing of the past.

During the same period, the Soviet Union withdrew its armed forces from northern Iran, gave up its territorial pressure on Turkey, and declined to provide direct support to the Greek insurgents. It withdrew the blockade of Berlin, failed to take military action against Tito's heresy, and watched while the Korean invasion was thrown back. The U.S.S.R. acquiesced in an armistice in Indo-China, and was denied when it asserted its interests in Konigsberg, Libya, the Dardanelles, the Ruhr, Berlin, and the occupation of Japan.

Whether Soviet expansion under Joseph Stalin was "defensive" or "offensive," whether it was ideologically or strategically motivated, or whether, in the end, it would be counted as an asset or a liability for Russia—these questions must be left to others, and to a record which is not yet written.

But on the record, the plain fact is that by the end of the first stage of the cold war the Soviet Union was still in control of those areas which were under control of the Red Army when the occupation lines were drawn at the close of World War II, with the exception of northern Iran.

And on the record, the plain fact is that by the end of the first stage of the cold war, Europe was recovering from World War II, the Western world had come together in an unprecedented military defense alliance, the United Nations had rallied to the defense of Korea, and the Soviet Union had induced the United States to prepare for the containment of further explanation by an elaborate ring of defense arrangements backed by military hardware.

Diplomatic action was unable to regain territories controlled by armies in the field. But diplomatic action could draw a line against new aggression—and did.

CHAPTER THREE

The Price of Containment

When Senator Vandenberg advised President Truman to "scare hell out of the country" if he wanted Congress to approve aid to Greece and Turkey, he probably was on sound political ground. It may well have been the precondition for bipartisan support of the Truman Doctrine. But there was an unforeseen price—a price which, as things turned out, would bedevil the government and the public for more than a decade ahead.

To win the support of an unprepared public and a reluctant Congress in what was, in fact, a desperate military situation, President Truman seemed to pitch his case for the defense of freedom on a *negative, military, and purely anti-Communist basis.* In point of fact, he did not. The request he made was for *economic* aid to Turkey, and for part-economic, part-military aid to Greece. In his message to Congress, Truman specifically concluded: "I believe that our help should be primarily through economic and financial aid which is essential to economic stability and orderly political processes."

This was the conviction and intent of the State Department staff which elaborated the Truman Doctrine. But it was blurred by the general tone of the speech, by the thunder of the military threat, by the overpowering image of a predatory Soviet Union sponsoring an insurrection in clearly strategic territory, and by the way in which it was reported in the press.

Truman's success in scaring hell out of the country established a tone that was to be followed for over a decade. For the next thirteen years United States officials annually debated whether the appeal to Congress for "foreign aid" funds should be presented negatively against the threat of aggressive Communism—or cast positively as a tool for economic and social progress abroad. For thirteen years it was decided in the end to make the negative pitch.

Along the road several convictions, rightly or wrongly, became imbedded in United States government thinking: that the Congress prefers military aid to economic aid; and that the latter should therefore be wrapped up in military aid legislation and justified primarily on anti-Communist grounds; and that the Congress and the public will respond better to an immediate threat than to a more distant opportunity. So it was that the historic decision to help other peoples to help themselves, deeply rooted in moral purpose and at once serving national interest and high ideal, was stuffed into the uniform of an anti-Communist crusade.

What's more, the Greek government in power at the birth of the Truman Doctrine was reactionary, inefficient, and corrupt, and Turkey at the time could hardly pass muster as a full-blown democracy. There were no illusions about this in Washington. The facts were that these governments were in power and were legitimate; they were fighting or prepared to fight against Soviet aggression and Soviet-directed rebellion. The choice was to help them or to look the other way. But it was an unhappy precedent for United States aid. From that day forward the world was never sure of the motives for United States support, nor of the credentials required to qualify for it.

Thus the defensive tone of the Truman Doctrine and

the dubious colors of the first beneficiaries of extraordinary United States aid were to prompt some nagging questions. Did the United States government think that military aggression was the whole of communism? Was it concerned only with strategic real estate and not with people? Was it the world-wide defender of the *status quo,* the automatic friend of every foreign reactionary provided he is anti-Communist and ready to fight? What, pray, is the United States definition of "free" world?

These and like questions would bother many an American and non-American for years to come. They would bring many a strange bedfellow to the support of "foreign aid." They would give rise to some bad jokes about importing Communists to insure United States assistance, and would befog the whole question of this country's purpose in the postwar world.

But perhaps the highest price of the policy of containment was that it was too easy to understand. The Russian Communists—talking, looking, and acting like perpetual enemies of the United States—were expanding by the use and threat of military power. Our policy therefore was to oppose power with power at all strategic points and thus contain the Soviet Union within the area it already controlled. Difficult, dangerous, and costly, to be sure, but easy to understand.

The trouble is that this policy helped to project a simplistic version of the affairs of a world in which there were Good Guys and Bad Guys. It induced a kind of fixation with Soviet military intentions around the periphery of the Communist bloc, permitting the Communists to focus our attention on crises of their choosing. It provided an easy answer to what is wrong, serving to obscure great events and radical changes remaking the world. It offered a kind of black-or-white criterion which Americans tend to seek for judging a policy, an action, or even the loyalty of a government official.

The impression of a world completely dominated by two super-states locked in a head-to-head confrontation, suggested by the doctrine of containment, became so firmly implanted in the national consciousness that it still persisted in the eary 1960s. This was part of the story—but only a part. It did not, for example, take into account the Asian and African revolutions, the massive social transformations almost everywhere, the relentless impact of technology on society, the emerging new international communities, or the rapid changes going on within the Communist world. All these were to be drowned out by the clamor of conflict between the colossi.

This was the price of the doctrine of containment.

CHAPTER FOUR

From Containment to Liberation—and Back Again

In early 1953 there was reason to suspect that the cold war was about to enter a new phase.

The Soviet decision to foster armistice negotiations in Korea may have had a number of mutually reinforcing motivations. Certainly Stalin did not relish the possibility of coming to the aid of his Chinese ally, which he was treaty-bound to do, in the event the Korean action led to war between the United States and China. Looking back from later years, it is permissible to wonder whether Stalin liked the idea of Chinese intervention in Korea at all. He certainly would not have liked it if he had suspected the coming competition with China for tutelage of his North Korean client.

Even a stubborn and obtuse man might well wonder whether it was time to change a policy which had brought about the Truman Doctrine, the Marshall Plan, the Berlin Airlift, NATO, and a network of military alliances girdling most of the Soviet periphery.

In any event, the decision in 1951 to end the fighting in Korea was extended in 1953 to Indo-China. Containment had had its intended effect.

Furthermore, a coincidence of history in 1953 provided added reason for expecting a change in the cold war: Dwight D. Eisenhower was inaugurated as President of the United States, and two months later Stalin died after twenty years of the blackest tyranny known to history. It is difficult to escape the non-Marxist conclusion that some of the characteristics of the first stage of the cold war derived from the personalities of Joseph Stalin and Harry Truman. Now that both leading protagonists in the cold war were under new management, new configurations could be expected.

But in 1953 still another event occurred which was to alter radically the structure of power which frames the cold war arena. On August 12, a little more than two weeks after an armistice was signed in Korea, the Soviet Union announced the successful detonation in the remote Pacific of "one of the types of the hydrogen bomb." The brief period when American nuclear supremacy was counted on to deter Soviet aggression had passed into history. Deterrence had become a mutual affair.

By our reckoning, then, the first stage of the cold war began in Iran in 1946, continued at full force until the military stalemate in Korea, and came to an end between 1951 and 1953. The first stage had been a period of move and countermove in which a reactive West, led by the United States, constructed a military wall of containment in a big-power confrontation around the Sino-Soviet bloc.

If the need for a change in cold war policy was felt in Moscow, it also was felt by the leaders of the new Administration in Washington. During the Presidential campaign of 1952 the Republicans described their own ideas for a "bold and dynamic" foreign policy. They advocated abandoning the "negative, futile and immoral" policy of containment, and instead would, "seize the initiative" in the cold war through "psychological strategy" and by "mobilization of the moral forces of the free world." President Eisenhower's election gave them a chance to put these ideas into practice.

A major objective of this policy, conceived and articulated by Mr. Eisenhower's new Secretary of State, John Foster Dulles, was to "roll back" Communism, especially by working for the "liberation" of the "captive peoples" of Eastern Europe. More than that, Mr. Dulles said that "we cannot tolerate . . . a welding of the 450,000,000 people of China into the servile instruments of Soviet (*sic*) aggression." Thus he indicated that the Communist tide was to be turned in Asia as well.

The roll-back of Communism, Mr. Dulles said, could be accomplished by a "peaceful process," adding that "those who do not believe that results can be accomplished by moral pressures, by the weight of propaganda, just do not know what they are talking about."

On his sixth day in office, Mr. Dulles indicated that "moral pressure" might be brought to bear on friends as well as foes. On that occasion, he told a television audience that the United States "has made a big investment in Western Europe on the theory that there could be unity there. . . . If, however, there were no chance . . . of getting effective unity, . . . then certainly it would be necessary to give a little rethinking to America's own foreign policy in relation to Western Europe."

The first big initiative under the new American foreign policy, however, came as part of the President's first State of the Union message, in the now-famous order to the Seventh Fleet in the Formosa Strait. At the time the Korean War broke out, President Truman had ordered the Seventh Fleet to protect Formosa against attack by the Chinese Communists. To avoid direct intervention in the Chinese civil war, it was also to prevent any attack on the mainland from Formosa. This order had been ignored by Generalissimo

Chiang Kai-shek, who proceeded to carry out hit-and-run raids on islands and coastal areas held by the Communists. However, in his State of the Union message in 1953, President Eisenhower declared that the order "meant, in effect, that the United States Navy was required to serve as a defensive arm of Communist China," and he therefore was "issuing instructions that the Seventh Fleet no longer be employed to shield Communist China."

This move was described officially as an act to "deneutralize Formosa" and to "unleash Chiang Kai-shek." It soon appeared, however, that its purpose lay in the realm of "psychological strategy." On the day after the delivery of the President's message several United States Senators raised questions about the meaning of the President's new order to the Seventh Fleet. Did it imply United States support for an invasion of the mainland? If Chiang Kai-shek invaded and then appeared to be losing ground, would the United States come to his aid? Senator William F. Knowland of California took the floor to chide his colleagues for asking such questions. He reminded them that this country was involved in psychological warfare and that the whole purpose was to keep the enemy guessing. To answer such questions as were being asked on the Senate floor would give away the whole game.

With some reluctance, the United States Senators suppressed their curiosity. But Senator Knowland's explanation was not good enough for some members of the British House of Commons, who pressed the same sort of questions on Foreign Minister Anthony Eden. Nor was it good enough for others in Europe, India, and elsewhere, who also raised cries of alarm. These soon died down, however, as evidence accumulated that Chiang Kai-shek was far from having the intention or the capacity to invade Mainland China—evidence which probably came as no great surprise to Mao Tse-tung. It seemed that, indeed, it was not the United States Seventh Fleet which had prevented his launching a full-scale attack.

The next initiative under the new Administration's cold war policy was the so-called Captive Peoples Resolution. According to advance notices, this was to be the kick-off in the campaign of "liberation" in Eastern Europe. Or so it was suggested in the initial publicity.

By the time the Administration proposed a text, however, the Captive Peoples Resolution looked more like an endorsement of wartime agreements and a denunciation of Soviet violations, and was unworkable politically. The Republicans would not vote for it unless it denounced the wartime treaties and by implication the Americans who made them; and the Democrats would not vote for it if it did. Senator Taft tried his hand at a compromise version which turned out to please no one but himself. Then, in the midst of this stalemate, came the news of the death of Stalin, and the whole matter of the Captive Peoples Resolution was buried quietly to avoid any danger of "rocking the boat" at such a delicate moment.

For the next several years there were no particularly noticeable United States attempts "to seize the initiative" in the cold war—except, perhaps, for Mr. Dulles's extraordinary and unsuccessful effort to pressure France into joining the European Defense Community. The "agonizing reappraisal" of United States policy toward Europe, which he threatened at the time, has since become a part of the American idiom, but it failed to persuade the French Parliament to merge French armed forces with those of the rest of Western Europe.

Toward the end of his first year in office, President Eisenhower caught the world's imagination with his offer of United States co-operation with other nations to foster the development of peaceful uses of atomic energy, though it was never claimed that this would provide any momentum for rolling back Communism.

Whatever else may have inhibited the Eisenhower Administration during the early part of its stewardship, the leading members of Mr. Eisenhower's party did little to encourage "bold and dynamic" actions. Senator John W. Bricker returned to his old crusade for the "Bricker Amendment" to the Constitution, which would have made it virtually impossible for the United States to enter into any international agreement of any kind.

Senator Robert Taft—"Mr. Republican" and Majority Leader—gave public voice to his doubts about the possibility of maintaining the free world alliance at all, and practically wrote off the United Nations as a useful international body.

But most disruptive of all, Senator Joseph McCarthy in effect declared war on the Department of State and thoroughly demoralized the United States Information Agency. He humiliated the nation by bullying the State Department into sanctioning the burning of books in United States libraries abroad, and distracted incredulous allies by sponsoring the shenanigans of Messrs. Cohn and Schine, foot-loose in Europe.

The Administration, it seemed, was under seige in a private cold war with leading members of its own party. Such an atmosphere was unlikely to help Mr. Dulles devise an effective "psychological strategy," much less to "mobilize the moral force" of the free world. In any event, as things went along, the new Administration returned emphatically to what had been called the "negative, futile, and immoral" policy of containment.

In the course of a few years, the Eisenhower Administration engineered the new South East Asia Treaty Organization, which pledged mutual defense of this area by the United States, the United Kingdom, France, Australia, New Zealand, Pakistan, the Philippines, and Thailand. It sought unsuccessfully to form a Middle East defense organization in the eastern Mediterranean, and settled for the Bagdad Pact, which the United States did not join, but which brought together the United Kingdom, Turkey, Iraq, Pakistan, and Thailand. The nation signed new defense agreements with Formosa, Viet-Nam, Korea, and Japan; helped bring Germany into NATO; and agreed to provide military aid to Pakistan, Iran, Cambodia, and Guatemala. The Administration announced the military doctrine of "massive retaliation," and sponsored a Congressional resolution which granted authority to the President to use force in the Formosa Strait if the Chinese Communists seemed to be launching a full-scale attack on Taiwan. Thus the doctrine of containment not only was embraced by the Eisenhower Administration, but stretched to its ultimate conclusion.

This essentially military view of the cold war was documented further by the composition of the Mutual Security Program, which had replaced the Marshall Plan as the vehicle for United States military, economic, and technical assistance to other nations. In the first Mutual Security Program presented to the Congress by the new Administration, 90 per cent of the funds requested were for military and defense-related purposes. Before long the aid program was being administered by a former Republican Congressman from Ohio, a law partner of Senator Taft, who took the general position that his primary task was to get the United States out of the aid business as quickly as possible. In the meantime, aid of any kind would be extended for only one purpose: to counter a direct threat of military aggression by a Communist nation. And for no other reason.

While United States policy, after a fitful stab at "seizing the initiative," reverted almost violently to the doctrine of containment, the Soviet Union was adjusting to the end of the age of Stalin. How tearing an adjustment that was to be would only be apparent in later years. But several things must be said about the change of regime in Moscow.

First, the Soviet Union by 1953 had made a remarkable recovery from the devastation of war—at a terrible price. At the end of the war the Soviet Union was under the personal control of a man who believed that aggressive Nazism was simply an advanced stage of capitalism and that it would return again to attack the "socialist camp." At the great victory dinner in the Kremlin, Stalin exhorted his officers to prepare for the next war without pausing to catch their breath; the economy would be driven at forced draft to rebuild Soviet war industry and the Russian people would have to endure their privations and their pent-up needs. During the next six years great purges were carried out in the Ukraine and elsewhere. The forced-labor camps were swollen with both German prisoners and Russian citizens taken away in the night; police terror reached its apogee. The state bureaucracy was terrorized and the party machinery was reduced to the role of carrying out the orders of Stalin, the all-powerful personal tyrant driving a nation to the limits of physical endurance to restore the heavy industry on which Soviet military capacity depends. Just before he died, Stalin exposed the fantastic "Doctors' Plot," an alleged conspiracy by Kremlin doctors to poison most of the high command of the armed forces. At the same time a hysterical campaign was whipped up against "spies," "traitors," "'cosmopolitans," and Jews. Russia, it seemed, was on the edge of another Great Purge. This was the mood when Stalin died. Things were so bad that the "collective leadership" which took over the Soviet Union pleaded at once with the Russian people to resist "panic and disarray."

Second, the Soviet system has no provision for orderly accession to power. It took both Stalin and Khrushchev years to eliminate their rivals and consolidate their positions. Khrushchev did it in four. But during that time the Soviet Union was ruled by a group in which no one man held a dictatorial position. During the period when Malenkov was prime minister it appeared that the Communist Party would be subordinated to the Soviet State; Khrushchev apparently was about to be dismissed as First Secretary in 1957 when he reversed the decision in a dramatic meeting of the Central Committee. When Khrushchev emerged triumphant, the members of the "anti-Party group" were not liquidated but merely disgraced and sent off to do minor jobs. The only known casualty of the bitter struggle for succession was Lavrenti Beria, the head of the secret police and the only man with the physical resources to do in the others. He was arrested by the collective group soon after Stalin's death and secretly executed by a firing squad, according to the announced version.

Third, there was a marked liberalization of domestic policy—relative, that is, to the fanatical tyranny of the old regime. The role of the secret police was demoted and terror no longer dominated Soviet life. More consumer goods of better quality began to reach the stores, people returned in large numbers from the forced-labor camps, and economic administration was decentralized. The tight restrictions on creative expression were lifted in 1953, then checked, lifted again in 1956, and checked again. At the end of these two "thaws" Soviet writers had been told in no uncertain terms that they were not free to criticize the Communist Party, the Russian state, or Soviet society as such. But they could write about people, about life, about human problems, even about love. Some years later a famous French photographer visited Moscow and met with groups of Russian photographers. On two previous visits they had lectured him drearily about "socialist realism"; now they were anxious to talk about "subjectivity" in photography.

Apparently the post-Stalin Russian leaders were convinced that the Soviet people needed a release from terror. How badly they must have needed it was suggested by the release in 1960 of the Russian motion picture *Clear Sky*. In this extraordinary political document, the death of Stalin is depicted as the end of a reign of terror, a liberation of the Russian spirit, a return to reason, a fresh breeze which literally melted the ice, cleared the sky of threatening clouds, and brought back the bright colors to nature itself.

Between the death of Stalin and the end of 1955 there were moves on the international front which seemed to be clearing the skies of cold war as well. Russian claims against Turkish territory were renounced and Porkkala was returned to Finland. In the Far East, Port Arthur was evacuated. Soviet armed forces were reduced by over 600,000 men, and Khrushchev made a flamboyant effort to patch things up with Tito. Censorship of the foreign press was relaxed in Moscow, and agreement was reached to resume distribution of the United States government magazine *America* in the Soviet

Union; the flow of technical and cultural missions as well as tourists increased greatly. Finally, after ten years of deadlocked negotiations, the Russians agreed to a peace treaty with Austria, withdrawing occupation troops which had been there since the end of the war.

There were a few other hopeful portents on the international scene. The festering fight over Trieste between Yugoslavia and Italy was settled. In the Philippines, the Huk rebellion collapsed. And in Burma and Malaya government forces seemed to be getting the upper hand over Communist and other guerrillas.

In the meantime it already was clear by 1955 that the Russians were launched on a cold war policy decidedly different from Stalin's. The major direction of the new Soviet policy was put on display during a boisterous junket by Khrushchev and Premier Nikolai Bulganin to India, Burma, and Afghanistan in 1955. Ostensibly the second man on the team but obviously in charge, Chairman Khrushchev talked peace, coexistence, and the lowering of tensions. More than that, he made sensational offers of economic and technical aid—"without strings"—to the countries he visited and to all who were struggling against imperialism.

Perhaps it was not yet clear that the Soviet Union was emerging from its cocoon of political and economic isolation. But the impromptu performances of Nikita Khrushchev in Southeast Asia—his alternate joking and bullying of the press, his obvious flair for popular politics, his disregard for formality and dogma—revealed that another kind of man was sitting in Stalin's old seat. If the world did not see the difference, it was not Nikita Khrushchev's fault.

Some analysts prefer to think of Stalin's policy, though expansionist and based squarely on military power, as essentially "defensive," and of Khrushchev's policy, though essentially political, as "offensive." They point out that Stalin was concerned with acquiring control over immediately adjacent territory—areas of "core" interest for the defense of the Soviet Union—while Khrushchev leaped across such areas to join forces with anyone fighting "imperialism." Some of these analysts trace the change in Soviet policy not to Khrushchev but to Stalin—citing the latter's *Economic Theses* published just before the Nineteenth Congress of the Communist Party of the Soviet Union in 1952. In them Stalin argued for the first time that while the "capitalist" powers inevitably would war with each other in a dog-eat-dog fight for dwindling world markets, the socialist camp might be able to avoid involvement. The reason, said Stalin in effect, was that the socialist camp had become so strong that the imperialists might never dare to attack it. This "shift in forces" suggested by Stalin just before his death would be hammered upon by Khrushchev for years to come, and be used by many to explain the behavior of the Soviet Union until 1960.

But in 1955 the Khrushchevian line was the "relaxation of tensions." And the event which caused 1955 to be called the "year of the relaxation of tensions" was the first summit meeting of the Big Four.

Since 1953 Winston Churchill had wanted an informal meeting of heads of state without a fixed agenda. So had some others on the Western side. But the United States and Germany, and sometimes France, took the position that the Soviet Union should first show concrete evidence of a cooperative attitude.

Early in 1955 Moscow suggested a four-power meeting of heads of state. But that was just the moment when the

Western Big Three were about to recognize Western Germany as a sovereign state, end the occupation, take Germany into NATO, and expand Western union as an integral part of the Atlantic Pact. The West was not prepared for a summit conference until this had been completed, which was in May.

The Soviet response was to establish the Warsaw Pact, formally linking the Soviet Union in military alliance with its East European satellites and providing a legal basis for the maintenance of Soviet troops on their territories. That done, Mr. Molotov appeared in Vienna and unexpectedly announced that the Soviet Union was prepared to sign a peace treaty with Austria and withdraw the Red Army, which had occupied the eastern part of the country since the end of the war.

This was construed as an indication of a more cooperative attitude on the part of the new Russian regime. The foreign ministers' meeting which concluded the Austrian Peace Treaty agreed on the desirability of a summit conference, which shortly was scheduled for July in Geneva. Just before the conference opened, Premier Bulganin told a press conference in Moscow that his delegation was going to Geneva "to discuss frankly with the other great powers the most important international problems, to find a common language and by joint efforts to achieve a relaxation of tensions and the strengthening of confidence in the relations between states. . . ."

President Eisenhower endorsed Mr. Bulganin's statement, and added that the purpose of the conference was "to attempt . . . to change the spirit that has characterized the intergovernmental relationships of the world during the past ten years."

When the meeting settled down, there were four main topics on the agenda: German unification, European security, disarmament, and development of contacts between East and West. These were discussed for several days. In a nutshell, the West wanted free elections and a united Germany, free to choose sides or stay neutral; the Russians wanted a European security pact, the abandonment of NATO and the Warsaw alliances, and the withdrawal of American troops from Europe. The West wanted an internationally inspected reduction of arms; the Russians wanted an uninspected agreement. The West wanted recognition of the principle of self-determination; the Russians wanted recognition of Red China.

In the end nothing was settled. All these matters were referred to another meeting of the foreign ministers.

But President Eisenhower convinced a nervous world—including, perhaps, the Russians—of the United States's desire for peaceful solutions, and was acclaimed in the non-Communist world for a striking offer to exchange with the Russians "blueprints" of the opposing military establishments and reciprocal rights of aerial inspection of each other's territory. It would be another three years before the descent of an American reconnaissance aircraft in the middle of the Soviet Union revealed how generous an offer that was.

Specific issues in the cold war—Berlin and the reunification of Germany being the foremost—were referred to the foreign ministers to work out. And at least it could be said that the "atmosphere" was "conciliatory." The leaders got together around the same table, talked of peace, and agreed that their differences must never lead to nuclear war. There was an air of *détente* that was enough to give birth to the "spirit of Geneva," a phrase which immediately became a favorite one for Communist propagandists around the world.

In any event, it seemed that the new management in the Kremlin was off on a policy markedly different from Stalin's. By early 1956 it became official.

At the Twentieth Communist Party Congress in February of that year, Khrushchev did more than denounce Stalin for the "cult of personality" in a sensational speech at a secret meeting of the Congress. He also laid down officially a brand-new Soviet foreign policy. War, said Khrushchev, "is not a fatalistic inevitability." Things have changed so much, the new chairman said, that: "There are only two ways: either peaceful coexistence or the most destructive war in history. There is no third way."

So saying, Mr. Khrushchev came down hard for peaceful coexistence. Under this concept, not even revolutions would be necessary for the ultimate triumph of communism. In fact, the "transformation to socialism" in some countries might actually take place through parliamentary means.

Not that Khrushchev was giving up his one-world ideas.

"The existence of the Soviet Republic side by side with imperialist states for a long time is unthinkable. One or the other must triumph in the end."

And he already had said that while "peaceful competition will be sufficient," if "anybody thinks that . . . we shall forget about Marx, Engels, and Lenin, he is mistaken. This will happen when shrimps learn to whistle. . . ." According to Khrushchev, the memory of Marx, Engels, and Lenin would be honored by a Soviet policy based on this proposition:

> Our certainty of the victory of communism is based on the fact that the socialist mode of pro-

> duction possesses decisive superiority over the capitalist mode of production. . . . We believe that all the working people on earth, once they have become convinced of the advantages communism brings, will sooner or later take the road of struggle for the construction of a socialist society.

Even before the new doctrine was laid down as gospel at the Twentieth Party Congress, some informed people inclined to the view that the United States policy of containment could stand "a bit of rethinking." Indeed, the United States delegation to the United Nations General Assembly session of 1955 wrote a memorandum which was released more than a month before Khrushchev addressed the Russian party elite, in which it said:

> The present period of history may one day be recognized as a major turning point in the struggle between Communism and freedom. It appears to be clearly a shift in the cold war, in which economic and social problems have moved to the forefront.
>
> . . . We are in a contest in the field of economic development of underdeveloped countries which is bitterly competitive. Defeat in this contest could be as disastrous as defeat in an armament race. We could lose this contest unless the country as a *whole* wakes up to its implications.

To Secretary Dulles the implications of the change in Soviet policy did not seem to require any new awakening.

"We need not become panicky because Soviet communism disports itself in this new garb," he declared.

And whatever the meaning or potentials of the new Soviet policy garb, it was soon to be blurred by violent events which seemed to resemble an older pattern.

The Year Both Sides Nearly Fell Apart

The year 1956 was the year of de-Stalinization in the Communist world and the official proclamation of a new policy of peaceful coexistence. It also was an election year in the United States. Beyond that, it was the year when both sides in the cold war seemed to fall apart at precisely the same moment of history.

On the Communist side the story begins with Khrushchev's attack on Stalinism at the Twentieth Party Congress. Although the secret speech was delivered in February, it was June before an astonished outside world learned of the fury of Khrushchev's onslaught against the "cult of personality" and the "absolutely insufferable character" of Stalin. Khrushchev said that the dictator had done "untold harm" to the Communist Party and "tremendous damage" to the cause of the international proletariat. Meanwhile the impact spread slowly at first through the Soviet bloc. Talk was revived of "different paths to socialism." Some of the satellite Communists who had looked with favor on Marshal Tito's ideas of "national communism" began cropping up again—including Gomulka of Poland, who was released from jail and rehabilitated. This was just after three days of bloody rioting had been put down by Polish forces in Poznan. And when the rioters were brought to trial in September, the world was treated to a spectacle unprecedented in a Communist state: the worker told their stories in open court; they repudiated confessions extorted by the police; and they described out loud and in public the misery of economic and social conditions that brought on the riots.

But if this was surprising, there was a still more astonishing spectacle in store. A few weeks after the trial of the rioters, the Communist Party of Poland, which calls itself the Polish United Workers' Party, met to deal with important Communist business. On the eve of the meeting there were indications that ex-heretic Gomulka would be installed as First Secretary of the Polish Party.

Then, without advance warning, an extraordinary delegation arrived in Warsaw from Moscow, composed of no less personages than Khrushchev, V. M. Molotov, A. I. Mikoyan, and L. M. Kaganovich, accompanied, it was reported, by equally distinguished generals of the Red Army. At the same time Polish troops under the command of Soviet Marshal K. K. Rokossovsky were posted near the capital. Additional units of the Red Army moved into Poland from East Germany. This was on October 19.

By 2:00 A.M. on October 20 the uninvited visitors were on their way back to Moscow. Gomulka had faced down Khrushchev in long bitter arguments, snatches of which took place in public. At this moment Poland appeared to be headed toward socialism along a Polish path, and the Soviet Union could not or would not stop it.

Two days later there was a demonstration on the streets of Budapest. Marchers demanded a change in the Hungarian Communist leadership and the withdrawal of Soviet troops from Hungary. Police broke up the demonstration with gunfire, but it started again the next day.

The heartbreaking story of how Russian tanks ultimately slaughtered some 25,000 Hungarian Freedom Fighters does not need retelling. Nor is it necessary here to pass judgment on the paralysis of the friends of freedom who looked on while it happened, nor to add to such poignant sidelights as the one which led Salvador de Madariaga to dedicate a book: "To the memory of the Russian soldiers who, in October 1956, left the Red Army and fought and died for the freedom of Hungary." The memory of such anguished events needs no prodding.

What is worth recalling, however, is that the rising in Budapest led to the replacement of the Hungarian premier and the Communist Party secretary with men who belonged to the more liberal and more nationalist-minded school of communism, and brought about the appointment of two non-Communists to the Hungarian cabinet. It inspired the release of Cardinal Mindszenty from jail, and forced a Soviet offer to replace the satellite system with a "great commonwealth of Socialist nations"—all sovereign and all equal. For this brief moment in history, the ideas of Marshal Tito triumphed over the ideas of the Russian Communists, and the allegedly "monolithic" Soviet bloc suddenly came apart at the seams.

But at the same charged moment of history, the Western alliance also was proving to be something less than united. The central thread of that story is the zigzag course of United States relations with the new Egypt, which, by 1955, was firmly in the hands of President Gamal Abdel Nasser. The United States had been hopeful at first that Colonel Nasser would lead Egypt out of the poverty and corruption that finally brought an end to the debauched rule of King Farouk. Washington had been by no means shy in urging the British to go all the way in pulling out their troops from the Suez Canal Zone—which eventually was accomplished as a forerunner to the formal transfer of the Canal Zone to Egypt in June 1956. The United States apparently was still hopeful of bringing Egypt into a Middle East defense alliance.

It was something of a traumatic shock, then, when Nasser signed a deal in September 1955 to swap surplus Egyptian cotton for arms from Czechoslovakia. Colonel Nasser has said that he twice warned the United States that if he could not get arms from this country to modernize his army, he would turn to the other side. In any case, that is where he turned. And the prompt reaction in the United States was that Egypt had "gone down the drain." What was even more shocking was the realization that the Bagdad Pact had not prevented the Russians from getting a "foothold" in the Middle East, that the new Communist strategy of aid and trade could quite easily leap over boundaries tightly sealed by military forces.

Nevertheless, the United States made a move in December of 1955 to stay on the right side of the Egyptian regime. A tentative agreement was reached to organize British, American, and World Bank assistance to help finance the construction of the Aswan High Dam. Whatever its economic and technical justification, this project had become the all-important symbol of the new Egypt on its way toward a modern society—a flag of economic independence to fly by the flag of political independence flapping in the torrid air of the former Suez Canal Zone.

But six months later the United States changed its mind. Communist arms were flowing into Alexandria and it looked as though Egypt would become dependent on the Soviet Union as a market for its perennial surplus of cotton. The Egyptians welcomed warmly Soviet Foreign Minister Shepilov when he came to visit the Valley of the Nile. Egypt was becoming a base of support for the Algerian rebels fighting the French further along the North African littoral. Anti-Western propaganda from Radio Cairo became more and more shrill, and there were reports that Nasser was considering Russian financing for the whole Aswan project. These and other events were interpreted as signs that the Communists had accomplished what the czars before them had never managed, a decisive breakthrough into the Middle East.

In any event, the United States abruptly announced on July 19—a moment when President Nasser was in Belgrade on a state visit to President Tito—that United States assistance for the Aswan Dam was "not feasible in present circumstances." Officials explained that the High Dam project would require such a diversion of Egyptian resources that inflation would result unless controls were established which the Egyptians were unwilling to undertake. If this was the real explanation, the events which followed were striking evidence of the practical weight of technical arguments against political symbolism in the contemporary world. If the United States policy reversal was an effort to put pressure on Nasser to mend his ways, it backfired sensationally.

Whatever the intent, President Nassser struck back in the only way he could. One week after the United States announcement concerning the Aswan project, Nasser announced the nationalization of the Suez Canal and the abrogation of the international treaty under which it was to be operated until 1958 by the Suez Canal Company, largely owned by French and British capital. For reasons which now appear inexplicable, the Western world was stunned. And for reasons which are easier to identify, the three Western Allies were soon split wide apart.

With United States urging, Britain and France made several unsuccessful efforts to find a new formula for international control of the Suez Canal, including a resort to the Security Council of the United Nations. The Soviet Union did its bit by vetoing a compromise resolution in the Security Council, and by offering to send "volunteers" to help Egypt in the event of an attack from the imperialist powers.

Britain and France were angered by the United States role in restraining their response to Nasser's illegal seizure of the canal and at what they regarded as a lack of support, even in diplomacy. They felt deserted by their oldest ally in a moment of crisis, and their editorialists said so. For several weeks London and Paris were hardly in touch at all with Washington.

Then, on October 29, Israel launched a "preventive" attack against Egypt. On the following day, without even informing the United States, Britain and France declared they would separate the belligerents by reoccupying the Suez Canal Zone. This exercise began with the bombing of Egyptian airfields.

No one will ever know what might have happened in Eastern Europe if the docket of world affairs in late October and early November 1956 had not been so crowded. The world's attention was split at least three ways—between Hungary, Suez, and the United States Presidential election. But on the day when the British dropped their first bombs on Egyptian airfields, Russia was offering broad concessions to Hungary; and on the day when British and French paratroopers floated down near Port Said, Russian tanks opened fire on the Freedom Fighters.

It is dangerous business to assign cause-effect relationships to complex historical phenomena. But a skeleton chronology of ten frantic days in 1956 recapitulates the vortex of events set in motion by de-Stalinization in the Soviet world and by the withdrawal of United States aid for the Aswan Dam:

October 27: Under public pressure for reform, the Hungarian government takes two non-Communists into the cabinet —an unprecedented violation of Communist principles of organization.

October 28: The United States election is nine days away—with the incumbent running hard on his party's platform of "Peace and Prosperity."

October 29: Israeli forces invade the Sinai Peninsula.

October 30: Fearful that the Communist empire is splitting up, the Russians make a sensational offer to withdraw all troops from the Eastern European satellites, guarantee their sovereignty and national equality, and establish a "great commonwealth of socialist states."

October 31: The British and French air forces start bombing airfields in Egypt.

November 1: Ignoring the Soviet offer of concessions, the Hungarian government repudiates the Warsaw Pact, declares its neutrality in the cold war, and appeals for support to the United Nations.

November 2: The General Assembly of the United Nations passes a resolution urging an immediate cease-fire in the Middle East, with the United States and the U.S.S.R. voting together against Britain and France.

November 3: Secretary of State John Foster Dulles goes to the hospital for emergency surgery three days before the election.

November 4: The General Assembly asks the Secretary General to arrange a cease-fire in the Middle East; a new "Revolutionary Workers and Peasants" government takes over in Budapest; the U.N. General Assembly calls on Russia to withdraw its troops from Hungary; and the Red Army opens a full-scale attack on the Freedom Fighters.

November 5: British and French paratroops land in Suez as the United States voters prepare to go to the polls the next day to re-elect Dwight Eisenhower for a second term in the White House.

In the days that followed, Britain and France yielded to world opinion and accepted a United Nations peace force in the Middle East while Russian heavy arms carried out the Soviet decision to stamp out the Hungarian rebellion. This decision was made at the very moment when a war was breaking out in the Middle East, when the Western alliance was split apart, when an American Presidential campaign was in its final few days.

It was under these conditions—after Hungary withdrew from the Warsaw Pact and appealed for outside aid and after the United States made it clear it would not intervene —that the Russians chose between a punitive action which they clearly did not relish and the almost certain dismemberment of their empire in Eastern Europe.

Thus the Soviet bloc, shaken throughout by de-Stalinization, was held together by the same technique which put it together in the first place: armed force. Suddenly it had become clear that the Soviet "bloc" was not nearly as monolithic as most people thought.

The simultaneous Hungarian and Suez crises left both camps in the cold war weakened internally. For this reason neither could take much advantage of the decomposition within the other. Neither could reap any real gain from the other's loss of prestige. The shattering of Western unity over the Suez affair and the uncomfortable posture of voting with the Soviet Union against its oldest allies in the United Nations held at least one compensation for the United States: its popularity in the Middle East and the other former colonial areas shot up precipitously.

But things would never be quite the same again after the days of Hungary-Suez.

The Suez adventure was the death rattle of Western colonialism, a fitful throwback which marred but could not reverse the demise of Western empire.

The Hungarian tragedy wrote an end to the doctrine of "liberation" and "roll back." The carefully nurtured complacency of "peaceful coexistence" went down the drain, while the "spirit of Geneva" vanished into the thin air from whence it came. The cold war was off on another zig.

Prestige in the Skies

The internal and external stresses in the wake of de-Stalinization and the consequent Polish-Hungarian affairs plagued the Soviet Union for almost exactly a year, and at times it looked from the outside as though Khrushchev's job might be up for grabs. Dimitri Shepilov was fired as foreign minister and replaced by Andrei Gromyko; a radical reorganization plan was announced to decentralize the economic bureaucracy of the state; the Sixth Five-Year Plan for 1955–1960 was way off the track and had to be abandoned for a new Seven-Year Plan. And there were indications that the spirit of Stalin was not yet dead in the Kremlin. It was not until July 1957 that Khrushchev turned the tables on the anti-Party group and ousted Molotov, Malenkov, Kaganovich, and Shepilov from office. Lesser shake-ups followed quickly.

In the meantime Soviet scientists, whether they knew it or not, were about to offset much of the damage done by the Hungarian revolution. On August 26 Moscow announced the successful test of an intercontinental ballistics rocket, and a month later the Atomic Energy Commission announced a nuclear explosion in the megaton range, north of the Arctic Circle.

Then on October 4 came the world-shaking news that the Soviet Union had formally opened the Space Age by putting a satellite into orbit around the earth, a bit of history which the United States had expected to sponsor.

If the Soviet Union lost one kind of prestige by brutality in Hungary in October 1956, another kind of prestige was gained with a shot into space one year later. If the Polish resistance and the Hungarian rebellion against Russian control smashed the illusion that the Communist bloc is "monolithic," the sensational news of the first Sputnik smashed the illusion that Russian science would always be inferior to the science of the Western world. And since both sides insisted on treating the first earth satellite not as a triumph in man's struggle to master his environment but as an event in the cold war, it must be reckoned that the U.S.S.R.'s first Sputnik was a "propaganda" triumph of the first magnitude. In passing, it is worth noting that communism's greatest propaganda triumph had nothing to do with Marx-Leninism, nothing to do with ideology, nothing to do with deception, distortion, or propaganda technique. It had nothing to do with anything but the simple truth that Soviet scientists had built a machine that could be blasted into space, directed into orbit, and made to send information back to the earth for the use, or misuse, of man. And this material accomplishment of Soviet society made a much greater impact on world opinion than the dreary abstractions of communist ideology. It would be an excruciating twist if Russian propagandists were to discover suddenly that "truth is our weapon."

Meanwhile, United States reaction to the Suez crisis was expressed by the "Eisenhower Doctrine" which took the form of a Congressional Resolution. The point was to "deter communist armed aggression in the Middle East area," to erect a "stop sign" by making it plain that an armed attack by a Communist power would be "met, if need be, by the armed forces of the United States."

The Eisenhower Doctrine was well received in Turkey, Iraq, Iran, and Pakistan. But they already were joined in a defensive alliance under the Bagdad Pact and the United States already was supplying them with military aid. The new doctrine therefore did not alter anything in these countries. But reaction was violent in Egypt, Syria, and other non-aligned Arab states which had declined explicitly to join the West in defensive alliances and just as explicitly embraced a policy of "positive neutralism."

There was no great enthusiasm in Congress for the Eisenhower Doctrine, but after more than two months of debate it finally was passed. In essence it was a projection of the policy of containment into a dimension never intended by its originators: a unilateral United States commitment to defend against military aggression nations which were unwilling to enter into joint defense agreements.

Nevertheless, the wounds of the Suez affair began to heal slowly. Prime Minister Anthony Eden found it necessary to seek retirement on the grounds of poor health; his successor,

Harold Macmillan, promptly came to Washington to start patching up relations between Britain and the United States. The NATO partners began to recover from the shock of Suez and its aftermath in the United Nations. At the end of 1957 President Eisenhower attended the annual NATO conference to offer missiles for European bases, though the missiles were not ready and the Europeans were not too sure they wanted them.

By this time Sputnik II was in orbit. The historic Soviet "first" in space brought on public consternation, Congressional clamor, and warnings of caution from the Administration against imprudent reaction. The net United States response was an increase of $1,500,000,000 in the defense budget and the allocation of an additional $600,000,000 for space development. But President Eisenhower stuck generally to the theses set forth in his 1957 State of the Union Message: "Any program that endangers our economy could defeat us."

Zigs and Zags—Or Were They?

During the three years remaining in President Eisenhower's second term, the cold war (or, more precisely, relations between the United States and the Soviet Union) alternated violently between times when tensions were taut and times when hopes ran high.

Generally, it was a period in which the Soviet Union had overcome its nuclear weapons inferiority enough to replace a one-way deterrent with mutual deterrence . . . in which the Russians dramatically asserted their equality or superiority in advanced fields of science . . . in which the

Soviet economy was on the move again at twice the rate of growth of the United States economy . . . in which the Soviet aid and trade campaign was gathering steam in Asia and the Middle East . . . in which conditions were ideal for aligning Communism with the anticolonial revolt in Asia and Africa. It was a period in which the United States government concentrated on military deterrence, "fiscal responsibility," and personal diplomacy.

Khrushchev's foreign policy has been described as far more "aggressive" than Stalin's, more "internationalist" because he abandoned Stalin's preoccupation with the physical security of the Soviet borders and sallied forth to identify Communism with anti-imperialism everywhere. In any event, his methods were different from Stalin's, and he set them forth in a much-quoted passage from an interview with William Randolph Hearst, Jr., in late 1957.

> We do have the ICBM, but I tell you . . . we will never use it against the United States unless the United States starts things first. . . .
>
> We declare war upon you—excuse me for using such an expression—in the peaceful field of trade. We challenge you to compete in peaceful things such as the production of radios and televisions and vacuum cleaners. . . .
>
> We declare such a war. We will win over the United States. The threat to the United States is not the ICBM, but in the field of peaceful production. We are relentless in this and it will prove the superiority of our system. . . . We will outstrip the United States. And it will convince the people that we are right.

This is what Khrushchev had been explaining theoretically to the comrades of the Twentieth Party Congress the year before: "Our certainty of the victory of communism is based on the fact that the socialist mode of production possesses decisive superiority over the capitalist mode of production."

Secretary Dulles took note of this shift in Soviet strategy when he told the Senate Foreign Relations Committee:

> I believe that the collective security system and the deterrent power which the United States possesses have caused the Soviet rulers definitely to decide that the expansion which they seek cannot profitably be sought by military methods, and therefore, they are turning their attention more and more to other than military ways, and I believe that the risk of war has considerably receded.

Mr. Dulles did not suggest that the risks of Communist gains by nonmilitary means might be increasing, but President Eisenhower did in his State of the Union message of 1958, when he said: "This non-military drive, if underestimated, could defeat the free world regardless of our military strength. This danger is all the greater precisely because many of us fail or refuse to recognize it. . . ."

Tensions—Down and Up

As the Hungarian and Suez affairs faded into the background, tensions let down a bit. By early 1958 the United States was back in the good graces of Britain and France.

Domestic morale recovered somewhat from the shock of the Sputniks by the successful launching of Explorers I and II and Vanguard I. In the meantime the Soviet Union announced another reduction of its armed forces by 300,000 men and pulled its army out of Rumania. It also announced a unilateral ban on testing of atomic weapons and started a marathon correspondence between Bulganin-Khrushchev and President Eisenhower which—though mainly a rehash of old Soviet proposals—kept alive the prospect of negotiations and spoke repeatedly of the need to relax tensions and to live in peaceful coexistence.

But by mid-year in 1958 world affairs were anything but relaxed. The Middle East had been stewing for months in the juices of inter-Arab rivalries. Colonel Nasser suddenly merged Egypt with Syria to form the United Arab Republic; Iraq and Lebanon then formed the opposition United Arab States. A revolution in Iraq brought a bloody end to its pro-Western government and to the alliance with Lebanon as well. A confused revolt broke out in Lebanon, with apparent encouragement from Egypt. Little Jordan looked like a sitting duck. Into this maelstrom, the United States injected the Marines to keep order in Lebanon and the British sent back to Jordan the armed forces they recently had withdrawn. Before all this could be untangled by Dag Hammarskjöld, acting under a resolution of the U.N. General Assembly, there was dark talk from Moscow about "volunteers" —and a demand by Khrushchev for another summit meeting at "one of the gravest moments in history," which had brought the world "to the brink of disaster."

And on top of the Middle East embroglio, artillery from the Chinese mainland opened up on Quemoy and Matsu islands. Some two months later it stopped again—but not until the United States Navy took charge of landing tactics to put Nationalist Chinese supplies on shore, and not until United States pilots had orders to engage in "hot pursuit" of any Chinese MIGs interfering with the landing operations.

Then, at the end of November, Chairman Khrushchev made a threatening speech about his impatience to get rid of the "bone in his throat" represented by Berlin. In the course of it, he delivered what everyone had a right to consider a six-month ultimatum for a settlement in Berlin. As the United States, Britain, and France started to huddle on what to do, there was muted discussion of whether another airlift would do the job. Tensions were very high in the second part of 1958.

But in the early days of 1959 they began to slack off again. Anastas Mikoyan, Deputy Prime Minister of the Soviet Union, came to Washington on a "personal visit" to the Soviet Ambassador—with prior hints that his country would welcome a major step-up in trade with the United States. In the end Mr. Mikoyan did not arouse much interest in a new burst of commerce. But his deportment was correct and his words were friendly. Shortly thereafter Frol Koslov was in New York to open a Soviet Exposition in New York's Coliseum—a project negotiated under a cultural exchange program aimed at "better understanding" between the two countries.

By midsummer Vice-President Nixon was in Moscow to cut the ribbon of a United States exhibition, to "stand up" to Chairman Khrushchev in an impromptu debate in a model kitchen, and to tell the Russian people via television of the peaceful purposes of the United States.

Then came the big news that would dominate the world's thinking about the cold war for another nine months:

President Eisenhower and Chairman Khrushchev would exchange state visits. Peaceful coexistence was in the air again: tensions once more went slack, and the Berlin crisis began to pale.

Mr. Khrushchev's tour of the United States in September was so boisterous that the *London Economist* described it as a "cross-country circus." But after a quiet weekend at Camp David with President Eisenhower, the two leaders agreed that while the situation in Berlin was '"abnormal," there need be no fixed deadline for negotiation. This cleared the way for a second summit conference. Thus the spirit of Geneva, which died of the Hungarian and Suez crises, was reincarnated in the "spirit of Camp David."

It was at this point that President Eisenhower decided to commit his world prestige to an unprecedented venture into personal diplomacy. Nothing could have been further from the concept of diplomacy held tenaciously by the man who had served as his Secretary of State for over six years. But John Foster Dulles had died of cancer in May 1959. And in December of that year the President visited eleven countries in Europe, Asia, and North Africa.

There were no agenda, no negotiation, no treaties. But welcoming crowds were tumultuous everywhere. Nothing like the mobs awaiting the President in India had ever been seen, and warm currents of good will seemed to be rising against the tensions and fears produced by thirteen years of cold war.

In February President Eisenhower toured four nations in Latin America. The second summit was scheduled for May. After that the President would go on a good-will tour to the Far East—and climax this whole extraordinary venture with the long-planned visit to the Soviet Union itself.

"Overflight"

Nine days before the second Summit Conference was scheduled to open in Paris, Nikita Khrushchev startled the world with an angry but triumphant announcement: an American pilot had been shot down near Sverdlovsk, deep in the heart of the Soviet Union. The pilot was an employee of the Central Intelligence Agency. His mission was to take photographs of Soviet territory between Pakistan and Norway for the information of the United States government. And, as it came to light later, the now-famous U-2s had been making periodic "overflights" of the U.S.S.R. for some years past.

Nobody in the West knows what went on in the Kremlin for the following week. Between the descent of pilot Francis Gary Powers and the ascent to the summit there were no clear indications of what to expect of Khrushchev at Paris. Those who read carefully a speech he made at Baku during the interim thought they detected evidence that Khrushchev was in deep trouble—in his own mind or with his own party.

In any case, when he arrived in Paris, Khrushchev was conspicuously accompanied by a grim, silent, and omnipresent Marshal Malinovsky, Soviet Minister of Defense. And the Summit Conference was over before it officially started when Khrushchev delivered a personal attack on President Eisenhower which probably has no precedent in diplomatic history.

In the aftermath Khrushchev announced the inevitable: President Eisenhower was dis-invited to make his state visit to the Soviet Union. To rub it in, he held a press conference in Paris at which his violence and vituperation came so close to hysteria that he threw away most of the enormous propaganda asset that the American spy in the sky had placed in his hands.

Details surrounding the U-2 affair—the near-comic confusion in Washington, the extraordinary gesture by President Eisenhower in publicly accepting personal responsibility for an espionage mission—the astonishing world-wide United States defense "alert" on the eve of the summit meeting—these remain in the half-worlds of speculation and secret documents. Perhaps there never will be an informed judgment as to what might have happened at the Paris summit if the ill-fated "overflight" had not been flown when it was.

But Chairman Khrushchev chose, or was forced by his colleagues, to use this affair as an excuse for wrecking a summit conference which he had wanted for long and built up to carefully. The repeated talk of "peaceful coexistence," of a "relaxation of tensions," of "war in the peaceful field of trade and production," the goings and comings of Mikoyan, Koslov, Khrushchev, Nixon, and Eisenhower, the proposed exchange of visits between the leaders of the two camps in the cold war—all this was to go by the boards.

As heavy gloom settled down over world affairs a deeply disappointed United States President returned to Washington from a long and tiring mission of peace with nothing left but his personal dignity. The spirit of Camp David had gone to join the spirit of Geneva in whatever resting place is reserved for deceased political slogans.

On his way home from Paris Mr. Khrushchev stopped off in East Berlin, where he made a speech which was threatening, but not as much so as had been expected after the fireworks in Paris. In effect, Khrushchev said that the only thing to do was to wait and see whether the next President of the United States would be willing to let down world tensions and coexist peacefully with the Soviet Union. His idea seemed to be that the cold war should be frozen temporarily in the *status quo* until a new President took office in January 1961. In effect, that is about what happened.

Not that all was serene in world affairs in the months to follow. There was the embarrassing finale of President Eisenhower's venture into personal diplomacy when the Japanese government called off his scheduled visit to Tokyo because it could not guarantee his personal safety. There was the rupture of diplomatic relations with Castro's Cuba, bringing the cold war to a continent which previously had been spared it and which was less than anxious to become involved. And there was the wild and woolly Fifteenth General Assembly of the United Nations, in which Nikita Khrushchev stormed, heckled, beat on his desk with fists, and waved his shoe in a futile attack on Dag Hammarskjöld, his office, and what both of them stood for.

But the cold war contest between the Soviet Union and the United States was generally in abeyance from the time of the summit fiasco until after the American election.

When the United States electorate chose John F. Kennedy as the next President of the United States on November 8, 1960, the cold war was in its fifteenth year. It had long ago passed through its first stage, and perhaps was coming to the end of a second.

During the second stage, the Stalinist period of Soviet expansion was succeeded by a Khrushchevian period which can best be described as general political warfare. For its part, the United States, after a brief fling at "liberation" and "roll-back," remained in an essentially military stance.

Like President Truman, President Eisenhower knew

how to stand firm. They both answered fire with fire; they both moved troops when it seemed to them that only troops would do the job; they both supported military aid to nations on the perimeter of the Communist bloc. The main difference between the Truman Doctrine and the Eisenhower Doctrine was that the Greeks and Turks wanted United States protection and some of the Arab states did not.

On balance, Mr. Dulles appeared to feel that military containment expressed in legally binding treaties and backed up by the United States deterrent power was enough to secure the non-Communist world until moral force, with some prodding from him, asserted its true power. Mr. Khrushchev appeared to feel that there is more than one way to skin a cat.

Nobody excluded from presidium meetings in Moscow can be sure of Mr. Khrushchev's major aims during the period between 1955 and 1960. If they were to extend the writ of Communist control, then they failed—with the speculative qualification of Cuba.

If they were to weaken the Western alliance, he could claim no credit for the weakness that developed at the time of Suez.

If they were to wreck the United Nations, they backfired.

If they were to build the prestige of the Soviet Union and its "communist" system, he had some success because of the aid-trade program, Russia's rapid economic growth, the limited but decided liberalization of life in that country, and most especially because of her spectacular scientific achievements in outer space.

But on the record, the plain fact is that the Soviet Union in 1960 controlled only the areas it controlled during the first stage of the cold war—less Iran, eastern Austria, the Karelian Peninsula of Finland, and Port Arthur, from all of which the Soviet Union withdrew.

On the record, the plain facts are that during the second stage of cold war, none of the dreaded "weapons" and vaunted techniques of Communist expansion added a square foot to Communist territory; that wars of Communist or Communist-led aggression in Korea and Indo-China were liquidated; and that insurrections of Communist inspiration failed in the Philippines and Malaya.

On the record, the plain fact is that the free world did not break apart under Communist pressure; instead, it was more likely to unite.

On the record, then, the West had not been in steady retreat before the deadly juggernaut of Soviet Communism led by the masterminds of the Kremlin.

All of which brings up the tormented question of just what communism is, and just how the world of Communism came into being.

PART TWO

THE ENEMY AND HIS WORLD

CHAPTER FIVE

"Communism Itself" or Paradox Regained

There are few, if any, words in the English language more emotionally loaded than the word "communism." And not surprisingly.

The leaders of Communism have proclaimed their total devotion to the world-wide "victory" of their system and their total hostility to every belief and institution important to Western civilization.

The two largest nations in the world are being transformed forcibly in the name of communism, and others are held forcibly under its control.

Uncounted men have fought and died for and against it; uncounted billions of dollars have been spent to promote or to defeat it.

Communism has inspired the devotion and the hatred of millions, made and broken political careers, guided a wealth of conspiracies and goaded counterconspiracies against it. It has fostered an anti-Communist industry in America and filled the big stadium in Los Angeles to hear "Hollywood's Answer to Communism."

Communism stakes its claim on being a "science," and has spawned the occult counterscience of Kremlinology. Communism is the subject of a carload of learned books and a blizzard of ignorant leaflets. Almost everyone has firm convictions about communism, and the woods are full of experts. Yet almost no one agrees on just what it is.

If the corner policeman is perplexed about communism, he can take comfort from the fact that he has distinguished company, for communism and its purposes have confounded some first-rate minds.

Such giants of scholarship as Salvador de Madariaga and Sir Bertrand Russell have violently different attitudes toward it. Such distinguished artists as André Gide, Ignacio Silone, and Arthur Koestler have first embraced it and then rejected it. Such an honored statesman as Winston Churchill once threw up his hands and proclaimed that the Soviet Union is a "mystery contained in an enigma wrapped in a paradox" —and some years later Prime Minister Harold Macmillan wrote ruefully to Nikita Khrushchev: "I must confess that I do not understand your purposes."

Industrialists, journalists, priests, professors, politicians, and plumbers quarrel and quibble as to whether the threat of communism comes from its ideas, its dogma, its atheism, its economic system, its conspiracies, its armed power, its propaganda, its local parties, its diplomacy, or the gangsterism of the men who run it.

Small wonder that *communism* is a loaded word.

There are, of course, remarkably detailed accounts of the history of the communist movement written by Communists, ex-Communists, non-Communists, and anti-Communists alike. It's all on the record; and unavoidably the record begins with Karl Marx.

Karl Marx, a German who spent most of his working life in the reading rooms of the British Museum in London, was a philosopher. Like some other philosophers before and since, Marx was in search of the one blinding truth, the one sure answer to everything; the immutable laws of social life, the key to past and the future, the one-shot explanation of all history.

Scholars have tracked down Marx's indebtedness to French materialists, to Plato, Heraclitus, Democritus, and especially to Hegel, whose so-called "dialectical method" Marx swallowed whole and raw. According to Hegel's dialectic, every idea, or thesis, produces an opposing idea, or anti-thesis. The thesis and anti-thesis then merge into a synthesis. The new synthesis thus becomes a thesis which produces a new anti-thesis, which in turn merges with the synthesis that produced it, and so on. Dialectics is a flexible "method" which can be used to prove almost anything. And it is notable for the fact that it offers no moral values, no criteria for making a judgment on the ethics of a given idea or policy or action or event.

Hegel believed, or claimed, that the essence of reality is the spirit; hence his dialectical method was applied to the realm of ideas. But Marx concluded that the reality of the universe is represented exclusively by matter, which changes with inherent and fixed natural laws. Thus man, who is only a part of matter, is molded exclusively by the laws which govern matter. In Marx's hands the dialectical method was applied to the world of matter and was christened "dialectical materialism."

Hegel found his single explanation of human history in the inevitable struggle of national states for world domination —to the total satisfaction of his clients in the Prussian court, which paid him to think about such things.

But to Marx the single answer to history was found in the struggle between social classes within the various nation-states. He believed that the basic human drive, as with other animals, is to wrest the necessities of life from the environment by whatever processes of production man can devise. It happened that the processes of production were changing radically during Marx's life, thanks to the industrial revolution.

Marx also believed that human society, and its social classes, is merely the reflection of its material economy and especially its system of production.

Now, according to Marx, since the laws governing the behavior of matter can be discovered by scientific methods; since man is but part of matter and his basic drive is to produce material goods; since society and class struggle merely reflect the economic structure with its particular system of production; and since history is the story of the behavior of societies, the whole of history can be brought under scientific scrutiny. So Marx set out to study the economic system which caused the class struggle. He would thus discover the "objective laws" of human society, which he thought would unmask the secrets of history and open the future to scientific prophecy.

Marx was devoted passionately to the scientific method and much of his work was disciplined rigidly by it. But he also was a romantic and sometimes a mystical thinker. Above all, he was an angry man.

Marx was outraged by the misery, oppression, and squalor of the early industrial revolution in England, especially by the sight of children as young as seven years old working fifteen and more hours a day in crowded, dark, dirty, unsanitary conditions for starvation wages. This was the system of production to which Karl Marx gave the name "capitalism."

It was clear to Marx that men could not enjoy even a

degree of freedom unless they were released from bondage to the productive process. And he concluded that capitalists were bound to the production process as surely as the workers. The system forced them to accumulate more and more capital through profits. This, he believed, required them to compete with each other, which decreased profits and increased productivity. This process released labor and forced down the wages of those who still worked, cutting down on the number of capitalists and multiplying the number of the proletariat. Thus it would go, relentlessly, infallibly, until misery became unbearable, until the workers saw the reality of the class struggle and rose against the system which had brought about its own collapse by its internal contradictions. The workers would then set up a system of production based on social use instead of profits—a system called "socialism." Marx predicted that inevitably capitalism would lead to socialism, just as surely as feudalism had led to capitalism.

Philosophers and historians insist upon giving credit to Marx for his contributions to social science. Western economists long took seriously his theories of labor value and the business cycle. And Communists still have bitter arguments about points on which Marx equivocated, including the question of whether violent revolution is necessary to give the final push to the collapse of capitalism.

Even if Marx had been only a detached philosopher, his historical analysis, his effort to apply the scientific method to social behavior, would remain a major chapter in the story of nineteenth-century German philosophy. Even if he had been simply an angry man and left science alone, he might well have been listed among the great social reformers. It was the fusion of his passions for reform and science that set off the explosion.

Marx's approach to history and his basic theories have long since been destroyed, most devastatingly, perhaps, by Karl R. Popper in *The Open Society and Its Enemies.* In the end, not one of Marx's "inexorable laws of development" turned out to be inexorable. It is enough here to note a few anomalies which arose from the work of Karl Marx, the philosopher, who was also an evangelical reformer.

Marx was an atheist, yet founded a prophetic religion.

Marx avoided all morality, yet started a cause which has drawn millions because of its moral aims and its sense of social conscience.

Marx damned all Utopians, yet started a movement to build a society the end of which was described by Trotsky as one in which "the average human type will rise to the heights of an Aristotle, a Goethe, or a Marx. . . ."

Marx denied the power of ideas, yet produced ideas which had spectacular impact on the history of the next half-century.

Marx believed men could do very little to hasten the inexorable and predetermined "stages of history," yet unleashed a violent movement by strong-willed men to control the whole course of history.

Marx asserted the impotence of politics, yet his disciples built a system in which political power is all potent.

Marx believed socialism would reduce both the potential and economic power of the state, yet the first "socialist" state was run by totalitarian political and economic controls.

Marx believed the world revolution would begin in Western Europe, where capitalism had reached its most advanced stage, yet provided the battle cry for revolutions in pre-industrial Russia and China.

As Herbert J. Muller has pointed out in *Issues of Freedom:* "The ideas that have most obviously and deeply moved men have always been questionable, sometimes demonstrably false or absurd."

Marx himself easily could have concluded that Marxism was demonstrably false. His whole system of historical prediction had to stand or fall on his proposition that "capitalism" could not reform itself or be reformed by political action. However, this process actually began during Marx's lifetime, with the enactment of the factory laws in England. These established a maximum forty-eight-hour week for work in factories and eased the exploitation of child labor. Thus reform was brought about by political action, which Marx held to be inherently impossible. Misery was not spreading. The condition of the proletariat was being improved, if ever so lightly.

Eventually this process of reform would alter beyond recognition the system of production which Marx called capitalism. It began before he died, but rather than suspect, or admit, that this threw a shadow of a question mark over the whole body of his doctrine, Marx complained that the workers were losing their sense of class consciousness. Marxists spoke darkly of the "bourgeoisification of the proletariat." And Marx went to work with his collaborator Engels to produce an "Auxiliary Hypothesis" to explain the offending phenomenon.

The temporary easing of misery in England, Marx and Engels explained, was possible only because the exploitation of colonies permitted capitalists to continue to expand profits without revealing the internal contradictions of the system. Revolutions in the colonies therefore would restore the process of decay in the centers of empire and thus hasten the revolution in Europe. Marx was referring especially to Ireland, which he regarded as an exploited colony. But the Auxiliary Hypothesis could be applied to the whole system of Western empire. In this context the much-quoted Communist dictum that the road to Paris lies through Peking is not a strategic but a theoretical formulation. Thus the Auxiliary Hypothesis added protective padding to Marxian doctrine and explained why "capitalism" did not collapse from internal contradictions. It did, that is, until Western empires dissolved in the years following World War II, and with them, Auxiliary Hypothesis as well.

Since no society has yet been established anywhere which remotedly resembles Marx's vision of "communism," its record continues with the story of those who have called themselves Communists, who have exercised power in the name of communism, and who have served as the keepers and interpreters of the faith.

And the first of these, Vladimir Ilich Ulyanov, would be known as Nicolai Lenin.

Lenin led the Bolshevik Revolution in 1917, thus violating Marx's formula that the revolution would have to wait until conditions "matured" in the most industrialized countries. And he led it through three years of war against czarist counterrevolution and British, French, and American expeditionary forces.

Until his death in 1924 Lenin maintained that any deviation from Marxist philosophy would plunge the revolution into the swamps of "bourgeois-reactionary falsehood." He fought what he regarded as heresy and he banished the heretics.

But he was just as quick to denounce "formalism." In practice it was essential for Lenin to make his own contributions to Marxism, for Marx left no plan for political or economic action, not a clue about what to do once the revolution was an accomplished fact. And with the flexibility of a brilliant opportunist, Lenin proceeded to interpret, abandon, adulterate, and supplement Marxist doctrine. Notably:

Lenin abandoned the Marxist dictum that the job of liberating the proletariat "is the work of the working class itself." Instead, he provided the proletariat with a "socialist vanguard"—a disciplined elite of trained, professional full-time revolutionaries, the hard-core leadership of the Communist Party of the Soviet Union.

Lenin abandoned Marx's idea that the Communist Party would join with other workers' parties to lead the revolution. Instead, he placed exclusive control in the tightly centralized Communist Party and ruled out everyone else.

Lenin abandoned Marx's idea that the revolutionary class was limited to industrial workers. Instead, he opened the revolutionary ranks to the peasant class, which Marx regarded as bourgeois and reactionary.

Lenin reversed Marx's theory that politics are determined entirely by economics. Instead, he made politics supreme.

Lenin elevated the role of the "dictatorship of the proletariat" to the forefront of his doctrine. In Marx's thinking it had represented but a passing phase before the state began to "wither away."

In the name of a philosophy which proclaims the impotence of the individual will against the "iron laws of history," the iron will of Lenin adapted Marxism to the realities of the Russia of his time.

In the name of "scientific" communism, Lenin denounced dogmatics for the "pitiful role of meaninglessly repeating a formula learned by rote instead of studying the unique living reality."

Thus in Lenin's day "communism" was what Lenin said it was. And he defined it in many ways, including this: "Communism is the dictatorship of the proletariat plus the electrification of the entire Soviet Union." Nearly forty years later, with characteristic license, the Communist Party of the Soviet Union recalled admiringly "Lenin's great formulation" of communism as "Soviet power plus the electrification of the entire country." In any event, Lenin's original formulation was a far cry from Marx; but by then the science was known as Marx-Leninism.

The next disciple with the personal power to define and redefine communism was Iosif Dzhugashvili, known as Stalin.

The world has been treated since 1956 to sensational revelations of the extraordinary rule of this extraordinary man for more than a quarter of a century. But we are concerned here with the record of "communism itself." And before Stalin was through with it, some striking changes had been made:

Stalin turned communism inward to build "socialism in one country." This was rank heresy. Marx had taught that socialism was impossible except on a world scale, and Lenin had said: "We rest all our hope on the possibility that our revolution will unleash the European revolution." But since the European revolution simply did not come off, Stalin decided, doctrine or no doctrine, to go it alone.

Stalin neglected the international proletariat, promoted

nationalism, and during World War II he revived plain old-fashioned Russian patriotism. To Marx and Lenin this was a decadent, bourgeois concept.

Stalin inaugurated in the 1930s the first of the series of five-year plans which have shaped and dominated economic life in the Soviet Union ever since. It was the first guide to action for the construction of socialism in one country, and an addiction to economic planning is now considered a major characteristic of socialism. But such planning is wildly non-Marxist. According to Marx, the system of production—and therefore the economy and also society—is governed not by man-made plans but by inherent laws. Stalin did not launch his first Five-Year Plan without a struggle with his own colleagues. Trotsky ridiculed the whole proposal as "substituting the multiplication table for a historic perspective."

Finally, Stalin subordinated all doctrine that got in the way of his obsessive belief in the inevitability of an armed attack by the "capitalist camp" on the "socialist camp."

From roughly the early thirties to the mid-fifties, then, communism was what Stalin said it was. By then it was called Marx-Lenin-Stalinism. And it was looking more Russian all the time; for if Lenin adapted the universal doctrine of Marx to Russian realities, Stalin grafted on a deliberately revived Russian patriotism.

Then came Nikita Khrushchev to tell the world what communism is, or at least it is in the eyes of the Russian Communist Party. Not only did Khrushchev denounce Stalin's "cult of the personality" and remove his body from its resting place alongside Lenin's in the great mausoleum in Red Square, the Mecca of Marxdom. Khrushchev made politics supreme not just in the Soviet Union but in world affairs, and he roamed large parts of the world in the manner of a politician working the precincts. He also roamed the far reaches of the Soviet Union—as no leader had done before—to preach the virtues of hard work, good management practices, and the supremacy of know-how. He set out to build Communist prestige by national power and national accomplishment. Khrushchev insisted that war between socialism and capitalism is not inevitable; that "revolution is not for export"; that the victory of socialism might even come about by parliamentary means, with the victors "buying out" the productive facilities of the defeated capitalists.

Khrushchev traced his ideological lineage to Lenin—when it was convenient. He even quoted the scriptures when they were useful, but he preferred to make his points with parables from the Russian peasantry. Meanwhile he scorned the professional Russian Communist ideologists as "Talmudists."

As these words are written, "communism"—in the U.S.S.R., at least—is what Nikita Khrushchev can persuade the Central Committee to say it is. In the new Party Program written by a committee under the chairmanship of Khrushchev and presented to the Twenty-second Congress of the Communist Party of the Soviet Union in October 1961, it is said that the next twenty years will see the completion of the "material and technical basis for communism." During the next decade, according to that program:

> . . . the Soviet Union . . . will surpass the strongest and richest capitalist country, the U.S.A., in production per head of population, the people's standard of living and their cultural and technical standards will improve substantially, everyone will

> live in easy circumstances, all collective and state farms will become highly productive and profitable enterprises, the demand of the Soviet people for well-appointed housing will, in the main, be satisfied, hard physical work will disappear, the U.S.S.R. will become the country with the shortest working day.
>
> In the next decade [1971–1980] . . . there will be an abundance of material and cultural benefits for the whole population . . . The construction of Communist society will be fully completed in the subsequent period.
>
> The majestic edifice of communism is being erected by the persevering efforts of the Soviet people—the working class, the peasantry and the intelligentsia. The more successful their work, the closer the great goal—Communist society.

The eighty-thousand-word Party Program is shot through with remnants of ideological catchwords such as "objective laws," the "class struggle," "bourgeois doctrines," and so on, including the old Marxist saw, "From each according to his ability and to each according to his need"—at some distant date in the future.

But ideology aside, the program is crammed with hard statistics on production of steel and transport and electric power; on the value of efficiency in production, distribution, and planning; on targets for the building of houses and schools; on factory meals, medical care, vacations, consumer goods, social services, and other such practical matters.

Minus dialectics, the vision offered in the Party Program was one of a rapidly growing, technologically advanced, mass-consumption, superwelfare state "in which the dictatorship of the proletariat will pass away, self-government will be established," and "family relations will be . . . based solely on mutual love and friendship."

Despite the "iron laws of history," the way to the "magnificent edifice of communism" was indicated clearly in the Party Program: persevering hard work by flesh-and-blood Russians, including the "intelligentsia."

After the new Party Program was presented, Harry Schwartz wrote in the *New York Times Magazine:*

> Khrushchev undoubtedly regards himself as the embodiment of the Russian people's triumph over their former masters. In his person the Russian *muzhik* has finally ascended to the Czar's throne, exercising power with confidence that his peasant shrewdness—unsullied by useless learning found in books—is adequate to the task.

Thus in Russia the "objective science" of "historical materialism" based on the "iron laws of history" deduced by the "dialectical method" was interpreted in quite different ways by three very different and very individual leaders to create the present Soviet society. Poor Marx! As Mr. Schwartz concludes the above article in the *New York Times Magazine:*

> . . . We do not know who will succeed Khrushchev nor what the successor's doctrine will be. The historic record suggests strongly that both the individual and the doctrine may be far different

from the present master and the present orthodoxy.

This is to say that in Russia both the theory of "communism" and the practice of men calling themselves "communists" have been different things at different times and that almost surely they will be different again in times to come.

Despite this record, there are those who still insist that the essence, uniqueness, and danger of communism lie in its allegedly dogmatic ideology. A dogmatic ideology, we are told, has powerful assets. It provides Communists with a fixed point of view—a shared way of looking at the world. It persuades them that they alone know the "laws" of social development. It justifies sacrifice and supports morale by convincing them that they are the appointed agents of history. It permits them to predict the future and soothes them with the certainty that a communist world is inevitable.

Perhaps. But the record suggests that dogmatic ideology is a very mixed blessing at best. From the very beginning of the Marxian movement, ideological differences split Marxism into radical and conservative wings; then split the radicals into Mensheviks and Bolsheviks; then split Lenin from his closest colleagues on the very eve of the Revolution.

But the greatest trouble came when the Bolsheviks gained power, for they had to deal with the everyday problems of running a government. The faith required them to find doctrinal support for what they did, and the faith was subject to conflicting interpretation. When the dogma does not fit the reality, Communist leaders have to revise the doctrine or face the danger of losing power. On all such occasions they have chosen to keep the power and alter the doctrine by making it "more precise," as they put it. But not without internal differences which have led to some of the most spectacular struggles for power in history, at the end of which the losers stand accused of "revisionism" or "dogmatism," depending upon the position of the winners.

Some may prefer to believe that these struggles are no more than sordid fights among unscrupulous men driven by lust for personal power. But ideology has either caused internal fights for power or at least failed to prevent them. In any event the record shows that theory has been steadily revised, often after costly quarrels about the role and the meaning of the communist dogma which is supposed to provide cohesion and unity among communists. Even if Russian Communists always saw eye to eye on the meaning of dogma, ideology would cause trouble by the simple fact that they are both Russians and Communists. This duality is represented institutionally by the Party and the State, which are not the same thing. And the interests of the Party and the State are not identical; indeed, they are more in conflict than in harmony in important ways, because Party interests sometimes demand policies and actions which are harmful and dangerous to the State. Since the Party is in control of the State, and since the principal state organs are administered by trusted members of the Party, the conflict must be resolved among Russian Communists—and within the minds of individual Russian Communists who may simultaneously be officials of Party and State. In any event they are simultaneously subject to the conflicting pulls of Russian patriotism and Party loyalty.

The record suggests strongly that without abandoning Party goals, Russian Communists consistently opt for the national interests of Russia if they are in conflict with the international interests of communism, and for the parochial interests of the Communist Party of the Soviet Union if they are in conflict with the interest of the world communist movement. Ideology is enough of a problem to make it difficult, even within the inner circle, to know just what the Party line is at any given moment. An example of such confusion is the case of Professor K. A. Mokichev, head of the All-Union Extramural Legal Institute of the Ministry of Higher Education of the U.S.S.R. In 1960 Professor Mokichev published a pamphlet under the official seal of his ministry in which he attacked the "revisionist distortions of the Marxist-Leninist teachings about the state and the law." Specifically, he blasted away at the tendency of certain Soviet lawyers to insist on the concept that an accused man is innocent until he is proved guilty. This, said Mokichev, violates Marx-Leninism, which teaches that "without the guilt of the particular individual in respect of the particular crime, there can be no investigation, interrogation or trial."

Now any good Russian Communist would have the right to assume that this was the last word on the Party line. Not at all. A few months later the Party's semimonthly bible, *Kommunist,* tore hide and hair off Professor Mokichev for "oversimplifying and vulgarizing the fight against revisionism." And to prove their own ideological purity, the editors of *Kommunist* quoted the ever-handy Lenin: "Adopt without question everything in the literature and practice of the Western European countries which may help to protect the workers."

That's how tough it can get, even for a professional ideologist, to stay on top on the ideology in a given Communist country at a given time.

But the record also shows that "communism" is different

things in different countries at the same time. Perhaps this is not unrelated to the plain fact that each country has its own distinctive problems. The Chinese Communists, for example are both Chinese and Communists, like their Russian counterparts.

In any case it was a difference over ideology which led to the split between Yugoslavia and Russia in 1948, or so the true believers on each side claimed.

The uprising in Hungary was not at first a demand for independence but a fight between two groups of leaders, both of which claimed to be simon-pure communists.

The Polish Communist Party has not tried to break away from communism, just Russian Communism.

And the most spectacular failure of communist dogma to invest all communists with a uniform world view is, of course, the row between the Soviet Union and China. It finally erupted for all to see at the Twenty-second Party Congress, precisely because two groups of leaders had conflicting views of the world and how to deal with it. Russian ideologists and Chinese ideologists have been engaged for several years in a feud so mighty that it cannot be disguised. When Chinese propagandists support Albania, they really are attacking the Soviet Union; and when Russian propagandists attack Albania, they really are attacking China. Nevertheless, if the Russians attack Yugoslavia, it does not follow that they are befriending Yugoslavia's enemy, Albania; and if the Chinese attack Yugoslavia, they are not necessarily in agreement with the Russians. At least that is the way it was at the end of 1961 and the beginning of 1962.

It is not necessary, or even relevant, to speculate on whether Russia and China will or will not stand shoulder to shoulder on any particular world issue. But if they do it will be for reasons other than a shared interpretation of communist ideology. Reports have it that the Chinese Party is hard at work on an "Asian" version of the "universal" doctrines of Marx. Meanwhile Stalin's portraits came down in Russia and went up in China.

Thus there is nothing in the record to support the proposition that communist ideology has served to bind together the Soviet bloc or the two giants of communism. The contrary is true. To Khrushchev, Mao is a dogmatist; to Mao, Khrushchev is a revisionist; to Tito, the Russians are dogmatists, but to Albanians they are revisionists. Which is to say that in 1962 "communism," in both practice and theory, is different in Russia from what it is in China, and in both of them it is different from what it is in Yugoslavia. This raises questions about just how "monolithic" communism is within a country, a 'bloc," or an alliance.

Even before Stalin's death, Milan Djilas, the jailed former vice-premier of Yugoslavia, in his book *The New Class,* came to the conclusion that "Communism as an ideology has mainly run its course. . . . The world center of Communist ideology no longer exists; it is in the process of complete disintegration."

Late in 1961 Wladyslaw Gomulka, the Communist Party chief in Poland, told a Party meeting in Warsaw that there is no need for a central organization to guide the various Communist parties; that each Communist nation should follow its own national path. He suggested that Communist leaders get together for regional conferences from time to time to swap ideas, but this would be enough in the way of internationalism.

Edward Crankshaw said in his book *Khrushchev's Russia*: " . . . I should take more notice of this ideology if anyone could tell me what it is—other than an impressive doctrinal rag-bag full of bits and pieces of ideas and feelings (above all feelings), some of them constructive and good, others plain bad, others simply silly." And at another point, Mr. Crankshaw referred to Khrushchev as "the greatest revisionist of them all"—a Communist who makes new contributions to the definition of what communism is on the average of once a week.

Scholars disagree on the state of repair, and the current significance, of Communist ideology. Marx's prophesies clearly failed. Marx-Leninism clearly has been revised beyond recognition. Stalinism has been thrown in the trash can. Khrushchev is a pragmatist. Communist ideology has not prevented fights for power within or among Communist countries. No one seems to know exactly what communism is in any given Communist country at any given time. And the social ideals which attracted many people in the early days of communism have eroded to the point where Russia now bases its claim for Communist superiority squarely on the point that its system can produce better material goods at a faster rate than the capitalist system.

"We challenge you to compete in the production of radios and televisions and vacuum cleaners," said Mr. Khrushchev to Mr. Hearst. Between the two world wars, a whole generation of American writers inveighed against such empty materialism when they found it in Midwest America.

On the record it could be claimed that Communist ideology now amounts to no more than "I-can-do-it-better-than-you-can." In this sense, communist ideals have been turned upside down.

But the record also suggests that Communist leaders still cling to their sense of revelation, to the theoretical *certainty* that, somehow, communism will triumph everywhere in the end. This makes a Communist different from a non-Communist, and a Communist society a different kind of place than a Western society. And because of the lingering faith in the ultimate "victory" of communism, what everyone still wants to know is: Do the Communists really intend to conquer the world? And, if so, how do they propose to do it?

Professor Elliot R. Goodman addressed himself to the first question in his recent book, *The Soviet Design for a World State*. He examines minutely all the available evidence from Communist sources bearing on the vision of a Communist one world. He weighs this carefully against evidence of a rapidly changing Soviet society and its deeply eroded ideology. In the end Professor Goodman finds a continuity in the hard core of Russian Communist thought which leads him to conclude that contemporary Communists still cling to the "goal of the Soviet world state, the most extravagantly coercive, caste-ridden world state ever conceived in the minds of men."

His conclusion is supported, in part at least, by Mr. Khrushchev's repeated predictions to the effect that our grandchildren will live under communism.

Yet apparently no one has bothered to question seriously the technical possibilities of a Soviet world state.

How far, for example, could the Red Army be spread around the world to maintain order in a Soviet world state run from Moscow?

How many Russian administrators are there to go around?

Who, pray, would run what is now known as the United States of America? Uniformed men from Novosibirsk? or the five to eight thousand members of the Communist Party in the United States, which has far fewer members and of much less talent than, say, the Junior Chamber of Commerce of New York State?

If such questions have been examined outside the Soviet Union, there is no evidence of it on the record.

Leaving aside the administrative chances of running the world from Moscow, it is not necessary to quarrel with Professor Goodman's conclusion that a Soviet world state would be the "most extravagantly coercive" ever conceived in the minds of men. It would have to be, by definition. But the record should be searched for evidence of a practical plan, of some sensible strategy, for reaching the goal, for a goal is not a plan. A strategy is but a figment of the imagination, or at best a piece of paper, unless it will work out in practice. And a prediction remains an empty error if it does not come to pass.

It is evident from the record, that the communist one world did not come about in the spontaneous way predicted by Marx.

If Lenin's view of a communist one world, midwifed by communist conspiracy, could be called a plan, the record shows that it failed.

If Stalin's retention of the territory overrun by the Red Army in World War II was the start of a plan for conquest, it has not been followed up since.

Now Khrushchev tells the Twentieth Party Congress: "Our certainty of the victory of communism is based on the fact that the socialist mode of production possesses decisive superiority over the capitalist mode of production." And he predicts that everyone eventually will want to adopt it because, he says, it works better. Mr. Khrushchev may feel with total certainty that the fulfillment of his prophecy is preordained. But does this make it a "plan," a "strategy," a "design for a Soviet world state?"

Nevertheless, the search goes on for the master plan of Communist conquest, which many people seem to take for granted. The search goes on mainly at the bottom of that impressive heap of literature, or at least writings, bequeathed by communist prophets long since dead.

No one can accuse the Communists of neglecting their theory, or of neglecting to write it all down; it's all there in the documents of "communism itself"—dreams, myths, nonsense, contradictions, and all.

By putting together bits and pieces from Mr. Crankshaw's "doctrinal rag-bag," it is relatively simple, on the authority of communist theoreticians themselves, to conclude that the cold war is manipulated by dedicated zealots, brilliantly maneuvering and "orchestrating" their secret forces on a global chessboard—all within the framework of a master plan complete with strategies, tactics, priorities, and timetables.

Prolonged exposure to the heady vapors of communist theory can induce hallucination. Once under its influence, the critical faculties falter. At this point, the "monolithic" structure of Soviet society suddenly becomes an unmitigated advantage to the Communists. The greatest absurdities of Communist theology assume a mystical power. Colossal blunders are ignored, or chalked up as proof of the slyness of Communist strategy. Banalities are imbued with profound implications. And finally the United States is faced with the alternative of "total defeat" or of "taking the offensive" on every "front" until we finally undo the Communists, in some unspecified manner, to achieve the "total victory" of anticommunism.

In 1959, for example, a group of scholars at the Foreign Policy Research Institute at the University of Pennsylvania, after years of study, produced an apocalyptic version of Communist strategy of conquest in their book *Protracted Conflict*. In it they describe the role of the Communist "conflict manager" who "extends his evaluation to the performance of entire rival economic and technological systems. . . ."

"In this broader dimension," the authors say, "it is not sufficient to study a single leader, his character, his training and his strategic preconceptions. The strategist of global, protracted conflict must seek to gain insights into the society which he is bent on conquering: its cultural matrix, its institutional structure, its popular emotions and neuroses and its decision-making machinery. . . ."

"In protracted conflict strategy," the authors tell us, "five-year logistical plans are meshed with decades of the tactical movements of forces and the careful phasing of political, economic, psychological, and military or paramilitary operations" into "one organic whole of political, military and economic effort."

Happily, the record of "communism itself" shows that:

—*The "scientific" basis of Marxism has long since been discarded by events as well as analysis.*

—*Communist doctrine has been adjusted profoundly over the years.*

—*Communist dogma has provided the basis for divisive struggles among Communist leaders within Communist states and for violence and quarrels among Communist states.*

—*In theory and in practice, communism is different things at different times and places.*

—*The vision of a Communist one world apparently persists among Communist leaders, but several versions of how and when this would come about have turned out wrong.*

—*If there is indeed a master plan for the "total victory" of communism throughout the world, it can hardly account for the growth of Communist power and influence to date.*

Which brings up the question of how that *did* come about.

CHAPTER SIX

How the "Communist World" Was Built

In 1939, at the start of World War II, the Soviet Union was the only country in the world under the control of a Communist Party. Ten years later, thirteen other nations or parts of nations are lumped with Russia in what usually is called the Communist world, or the Communist empire or bloc. It covers one-fourth of the surface of the earth and includes one-third of the world populations.

The growth of this "empire" is said to be comparable only to the Greco-Macedonian conquest of western Asia in the fourth century B.C., to the Roman Empire of the second century B.C., to the Islamic expansion of the seventh century, and to the empires conquered by Attila, Genghis Khan, and Tamerlane. In October 1961 *Life* magazine took a long look and concluded: "The Communist movement . . . has been gaining land and converts at a faster rate than any political or religious movement in history."

The story of the expansion of Communist control is intoxicating stuff for anyone susceptible to the villain theory of history, the notion that all the ills of the world can be traced to conspiracies operated by the villains of the piece—capitalists, munitions-makers, Jews, Communists, underlings in the State Department, what-not. Uncover the conspiratorial group, according to this theory, and you have the answer to disaster, crisis, confusion, frustration, or whatever troubles you, including the graduated income tax or fluoridated waters.

The villain theory is, of course, attractive to all seekers for the Easy Answer, especially in times of trouble. In the Communist world everything that goes seriously wrong is traced to the war-mongering capitalist imperialists or to "bourgeois wreckers" infected with capitalist mentality. Even hard-core Communists who lose out in the intermittent power struggles may be charged as "capitalist spies."

To seekers for the Easy Answer in the non-Communist world, the villain acountable for all ills, foreign and domestic, is likely to be the Communist conspiracy to conquer the world. To support the thesis, it is first necessary to prove that the conspiracy is succeeding and that Communism is in fact sweeping the world with planned precision.

Happily or unhappily, the story of Communist expansion is marvelously suited to visual presentation. In 1961 a number of film strips and motion pictures were in distribution throughout the nation, especially among fundamentalist religious groups, to "educate" the public by proving graphically that the Communists already are well on their way toward ultimate world conquest. By the use of maps and animated techniques, by selecting certain events and ignoring others, it is surprisingly easy to do.

In the "documentary" film *Communist Encirclement, 1961,* for example, big red arrows stab out across a technicolor map from Mother Russia. First they blot out a piece of Finland, then Latvia, Estonia, and Lithuania. Then Eastern and parts of Central Europe are engulfed, country by country, conquest by conquest, in rapid-fire order, until Western

Europe looks surely doomed. Next the whole of China is washed in the red tide, and the menacing arrows point their daggers deep into South and Southeast Asia, the Middle East, and Africa. Finally, the red center of Castro's Cuba is shown as the pivot for Communist tentacles wrapped halfway around Latin America and the United States as well.

Thus the United States, by visual proof, is encircled by Communism. And the anonymous film narrator explains that each stage of expansion is in strict pursuit of Lenin's "master plan," his "blueprint" for world conquest.

One is tempted at this point to think back to one of the Russian "masters of conflict management." Having penetrated the "cultural matrix" of the victim nation, secure in his knowledge of its "decision-making machinery" and its "popular emotions and neuroses," he maneuvers his "political, economic, psychological and military and paramilitary forces" at the right time and in the right place until Communism has enslaved another nation. This task completed, one can imagine him turning eagerly to the next nation, which to him is but "a mere salient to be reduced"—or even to a whole continent which is but "a mere flank to be turned" in *Protracted Conflict*. Patient fellow that he is, we can assume him to be undaunted by the prospect of meshing "five-year logistical plans with decades of tactical movement of forces" as he tackles the next foredoomed victim.

Fortunately, the record of how Communism spread to thirteen nations is not quite so frightening as suggested by the authors of *Protracted Conflict* or the producers of *Communist Encirclement*. Film producers and graphic artists in Russia have, of course produced visual proof of "capitalist encirclement" of the Soviet Union with similar animated maps and with simple posters showing United States military alliances and air bases ringing the U.S.S.R. They are very impressive, too.

In any case, a shorthand record of the growth of the Communist world might well be reviewed in a less dramatic fashion.

How Communism Came to Russia

In early 1917 Russia was at war and had suffered grave defeats at the front. Behind the lines there were serious food shortages and mass hunger. And the machinery of state was breaking down, not only in the cities but in the countryside, where peasants were wont to murder the landlords and divide their property.

When the Russian Revolution broke out at the end of February, it was all over in a few days. It began with spontaneous street disturbances in Petrograd as people sought food from empty stores. There was no organization, no leader, no revolutionary program. But as the crowd grew, the police disappeared—and the crowds grew some more. The soldiers were unable or unwilling to clear the streets. A feeling of anarchy took over the city. Within a couple of days the whole administrative machinery of imperial Russia simply dissolved. The czar abdicated and left with his family. Control of the nation passed to a Provisional Government, under Alexander Kerensky, appointed by a committee of the Parliament—plus the Petrograd Soviet, a council of workers and soldiers thrown together suddenly without a program of its own or very clear leadership. As Herbert Muller has said in *Uses of the Past:* "The Russian Revolution began as the easiest, most painless cataclysm in all history."

Nothing could have come as a greater surprise to the Marxist revolutionaries. They did not plan, lead, or even believe in the Russian Revolution. Trotsky admitted later on: "The most revolutionary party which human history until this time had ever known was nevertheless caught unawares by the events of history. . . ." Trotsky at the time was resident in New York. Lenin was living in Geneva.

For the following eight months the Russian people had the only would-be democratic government in their history to date. But the division of authority between the Provisional Government and the nongovernmental Soviet was inherently unworkable. The war went on, and Russian losses mounted toward 7,000,000 dead. Hunger persisted, And, thanks to the foresight of the German General staff, Lenin came back to Russia in early April in the famous "sealed train" from Switzerland.

When Lenin got off the train at the Finland Station in Petrograd, he shocked his audience and his own colleagues by concluding a speech with the words, "Long live the Socialist Revolution!" He was the only Marxist in Russia who believed that the time had come to seize power. He was not even the leader of the splinter group called the Bolsheviks. But by sheer force of personality and oratory, and with the help of Trotsky, who later made his way from New York, Lenin finally persuaded at least some of the Bolsheviks the proletarian revolution could begin in Russia. Lenin had long been convinced that it was only the reactionary power of czarist Russia which had held back a revolution in Germany. Thus, he argued, a revolution in Russia would spark a revolution in Germany which, in turn, would sweep through the other industrialized countries. And this would satisfy the theoretical requirement for an industrial base for the building of socialism.

On the night of October 24 the Military Revolutionary Committee on the Petrograd Soviet, headed by Trotsky, sent armed detachments to occupy the key points of the city. There was no opposition. By the next day all the members of the Provisional Government were under arrest, except for Kerensky, who fled, as the czar had done before him. In an account of the Bolshevik take-over of the Russian Revolution in *An Illustrated History of Russia,* Joel Carmichael writes:

> The actual *coup d'état,* freely discussed beforehand, was child's play: against the general background of civic disintegration, mass apathy, and more particularly the utter incapacity of the Provisional Government . . . the Bolsheviks found it simple to apply a plan of their own. . . . The insurrection, was, in fact, a very flabby affair; its success can only be explained by the bewildering indolence of the Bolsheviks' opponents.

With the exception of some new Cossack units, the illiterate peasant soldiers of the Russian Army stayed with Lenin and his "revolution." Not that he bored them with theoretical excursions into dialectical materialism; he simply promised them what they wanted, peace, bread, and land. It was enough.

In any event, communism came to power in Russia not by winning converts, but by seizing key points with armed units and arresting the members of the existing government in the middle of the night. It had nothing to do with the iron laws of history, the internal contradiction of capitalism, or proletarian class consciousness. It had everything to do with war, hunger, internal collapse, and the fire that burned in the belly of Nikolai Lenin.

We often hear that the Bolsheviks were tightly organized, fanatically disciplined, and vastly skilled in the techniques of revolution. The record suggests that they did not need such formidable assets for a midnight coup which was no more complicated than dozens of such operations in dozens of countries which have been carried out successfully by militarists, rightists, leftists, and moderates as well.

Through the next ten years of war, civil war, and great confusion; through succeeding years of starvation, mass deportations, and massive purges; and on through the horrors of World War II, the Communist Party of the Soviet Union used the techniques of propaganda, infiltration, subversion, espionage, terror, and many forms of political and economic pressures against the Russian people. But behind them all lay the simplest and oldest technique of all: control of military and police force power.

It was a long time after the Bolshevik coup before communism was to have any great success outside the Soviet Union, despite abortive revolutions in Germany, Hungary, and Persia.

Twenty years after the Bolshevik coup in Russia, then, Communist control was still confined to one country. Despite all the efforts of the international Communist conspiracy, and despite the existence of Communist parties in many countries, Marx's prophecy of chain-reaction communist revolutions turned out to be false, and so did Lenin's.

How Communism Spread to Eastern Poland and the Baltic

In August 1939, for reasons which are irrelevant to this record, Communist Russia and Nazi Germany signed the Ribbentrop-Molotov Pact. Allegedly it was a nonaggression agreement, but it had a secret protocol which dealt with a division of the spoils of a war Hitler was to launch against Poland a few days later. Toward the end of the Nazi campaign in Poland, the terms of the deal came to light. As Poland was collapsing before Hitler's Panzer divisions and dive-bombers, from the west, the Red Army marched into eastern Poland and took over that half of a helpless country.

Then Stalin demanded military bases in the little Baltic republics of Latvia, Lithuania, and Estonia, carved out of Russia at the end of the World War I. The demand was accepted; resistance was hopeless. With his military forces already in control, Stalin later insisted that the Baltic states become full-fledged "republics" of the Soviet Union. They were soon absorbed, lock, stock, and barrel, a process which involved brutal transfers of Baltic peoples to remote regions of Russia, with attendant starvation, barbarities, and death. But "communism" did not "spread" to the Baltic states: the Soviet Union captured some strategic real estate by overwhelming military power. It did so under an agreement with Nazi Germany and at a time when there was no reason to fear military reprisals from another large power.

Stalin also demanded military bases in Finland. But unlike the others, the Finns refused. In the winter of 1938–

1939 the Red Army attacked. After an embarrassingly hard time with Finnish ski troops—who appeared quite immune to Communist propaganda and highly allergic to the prospects of living under Communism—the war was settled by a treaty which granted limited base rights to Russia in parts of Finland. It was an open-and-shut case of a big power opening aggressive war upon a small neighbor for military advantage which it could not gain by negotiations or intimidation.

Thus did Communism spread to the Baltic and half of Poland, under the aegis of the Red Army and by the grace of anti-Communist Adolph Hitler in the middle of a war. Thus did the frontiers of Soviet Russia come to approximate the borders of czarist Russia. Communism gained few converts and fewer friends in the process, though the area of Soviet control was extended. It was the end of the process of Communist expansion until the end of World War II, and it is worth recalling the general state of affairs on that happy occasion.

How Communism Spread to Eastern and Central Europe

At the close of World War II the Soviet Union was desperately wounded, a casualty of war, privation, and immense dislocation. Retreating Nazi armies had carried the scorched earth technique to its ultimate, annihilistic end. They had literally burned every building to which they could set the torch, killed every farm animal down to poultry, destroyed every means of transport down to wheelbarrows. The result was that the richest one-third of the Soviet Union was the most thoroughly ravished land in the history of human destructiveness. More than 20,000,000 soldiers and civilians were dead or wounded.

Britain was broke; more than half her merchant fleet was rusting on the bottom of the ocean; much of her industrial plant had been blitzed. London was full of great gaping holes where buildings had once stood, and those that were left were drab, dirty, and windowless. And much more important, the Empire, which everyone thought was the single source of Britain's great strength, was coming apart at the seams. It was obvious to everyone that Britain was washed up as a big power in the world, even to many Britishers who queued up for ocean passages to emigrate to greener pastures.

Germany was more a mass of rubble than a nation. Berlin, Düsseldorf, Stuttgart, Hamburg, Bremerhaven were great piles of idiot wreckage deep in the dust of powdered mortar and still pocked with the dying fires of incendiary bombs. The country was split into four zones of occupation. The only people who thought Germany could ever rise again did their best to make sure that she wouldn't. Everyone knew that Germany could never become viable as long as the industrial west was cut off from its breadbasket in the eastern zone.

France was not so bady beaten physically, but disorganized, exhausted, and demoralized.

For the Dutch, the handwriting already was on the walls of Indonesia, even if they were too stubborn to read it.

As for Italy, she was beaten, damaged, occupied; and, anyway, most people felt that her pretensions to power had been no more than the fantasy of a second-rate dictator.

Japan was in a state of national shock from the horrors

of Hiroshima and Nagasaki. Her armed forces were being destroyed; her "Co-Prosperity Sphere" was being disassembled; and General MacArthur was about to take over the liquidation of the political power. It was obvious to all that the best that Japan could hope for was that she would somehow manage to scrounge enough food for her bloated population to avoid mass hunger.

China was bleeding in civil war, and India, about to become independent, faced religious war and the stupefying fact of mass poverty.

The fact is that, materially speaking, the United States stood alone as the only great power left on earth as World War II came to its close.

With no physical damage at home, with an industrial capacity expanded by 50 per cent during the war, with a cruel but relatively light loss of lives—and with a world monopoly on a weapon of unheard-of destructiveness—the United States emerged from the war in the most pre-eminently powerful position of any nation since the fall of Rome.

But the United States, with almost indecent haste, dismantled the greatest military machine ever assembled and went all out to "bring the boys home." Within less than two years after the close of the war, United States armed forces had been chopped from 12,000,000 to 1,500,000 men. Equipment overseas was junked, abandoned, or sold for knock-down prices. Equipment at home was junked or stored or tucked away in moth balls.

A few sobersides—Averell Harriman was one of them—tried to protest the wisdom of all-out demobolization; but there was nobody to listen. The United States was riding hell-for-leather toward normalcy. And the Red Army was in occupation of Eastern and parts of Central Europe, still mobilized despite the terrible losses and devastation back home in Russia.

It is not necessary to speculate here on what motivated Stalin to keep control of Eastern and Central Europe. This record is not concerned with the *why* but the *how* of the extension of Communist control over Rumania, Bulgaria, Hungary, Poland, Czechoslovakia, East Germany, Yugoslavia, and Albania.

The Soviet take-over of Eastern Europe followed a roughly standard three-step pattern in the various countries, though the steps and circumstances varied, of course, from place to place. First there was a period when the occupied country was run by a genuine coalition government, always including the Communists. This was followed by an alleged coalition in which the Communists held all or almost all the keys to effective national control. The final step was the liquidation of all political organizations but the Communist Party, followed by a single-slate "election" and the promulgation of a "people's republic" along the Soviet model. This process was spread out over a two-to-three-year period in Eastern Europe.

Detailed accounts of the long and complicated techniques of absorbing Eastern Europe into the Soviet bloc have been recorded by several eyewitnesses and scholars. Perhaps the most careful account is given by Professor Seton-Watson in his *East European Revolution.*

The techniques were varied and unlovely: murder, arrest, torture, blackmail, falsification of ballots, hooliganism, strikes, lockouts, suppression of periodicals, whatever was needed. Behind the success of these techniques was the fact that the local Communists were in control of the internal points of power and pressure. Behind that is the fact that the local Communists, many of whom spent the war years in Russia and returned with Russian troops, were under the protection of the Soviet occupation authorities. And behind the Soviet occupation authorities stood the Red Army, on the ground or within ready call. Propaganda, infiltration, subversion—all were used, but all were used under the protective wing of Soviet military power, in place or at the ready.

All this occurred in countries disrupted by war, enemy occupation, resistance fighting, or invasion, or some combination of these calamities. Most of the old democratic political parties had been broken up or seriously weakened during the years of World War II. Most of the old political leaders, with a few exceptions, were gone or were faded from years of exile or underground existence. In short, there were no effective political or executive organs to oppose the imposition of Communism by Soviet authorities on the spot.

Some qualifications have to be made for the case of Czechoslovakia. Here there was a heritage of democratic rule between the two world wars; competent democratic leaders were on hand after World War II; and the Red Army was not in direct occupation at the time of the Communist take-over. But Czechoslovakia was surrounded on three sides by Soviet troops, and on the fourth side was the ancient enemy, Germany. Czech leaders were obsessed with the illusion that their only security lay in continued alliance with the Soviet Union. As in most of Europe, the resistance movement against the Nazi occupation of Czechoslovakia had been dominated by Communists, who therefore appeared as postwar heroes. When most of Czechoslovakia was liberated by Russian troops, Communists were put in control of the levers of internal power and influence—in the police, propaganda and other organs, including paramilitary units of street fighters euphemistically known as "factory guards." These levers were manipulated by Soviet authories until a blunder by the non-Communist members of the Czech cabinet opened the way for Mr. Zorin to show up in Prague and preside over the final turn of the screw against an ailing Czech President, who feared the revival of Fascism more than the presence of Communism.

The Soviet Union could have taken over the nations of Eastern Europe at any time after they were overrun by the Red Army. For reasons of their own—perhaps to minimize Western objections and to give the illusion that what was happening was an internal affair—the Russians choose to absorb the satellites by comfortable and gradual stages.

There is nothing in the record to prove whether the process could have been halted by anything short of war with the Soviet Union. It simply shows that at no point did Stalin take an irrevocable step; he could have backed down or side-stepped at any time. Beyond that, the record for Eastern Europe shows that a powerful military nation whose army has overrun neighboring territory can hold onto the ground it has captured. It proves nothing about dialectical materialism, ideological dogma, the influence of propaganda, or the power of "ideas."

Then there was the case of Yugoslavia and Albania, to which communism spread without the benefit of Soviet troops and Russian occupation authorities. Both had been invaded and occupied by enemy troops in the war. Both governments had fled. In Yugoslavia and to a lesser extent Albania, partisan forces fought the invaders under the competent military and political direction of native Communists. In Yugoslavia, with the help of Allied arms smuggled across the Adriatic, Marshal Tito's guerrillas fought bitterly and bravely against the Nazi occupation forces. They won the backing of the Yugoslavs for fighting the enemy, and the backing of the Allies for pinning him down. The same could not be said for the forces of General Draja Mikhailovich, loyal to the refugee king. He, too, was supplied by the Allies, but saved his ammunition for use against Tito's forces—against which, in the end, he was no match. In Albania there was no effective opposition to the Communist partisan forces once the occupation troops withdrew.

Thus in two nations—invaded, defeated, and without national civil authority—armed forces led by Communists and supplied from abroad took over control when the enemy retreated. Both had national Communist leaders, friendly to Moscow and the international brotherhood, of course, but not the hand-picked stooges of the Kremlin. And neither was a member of the Soviet bloc at the end of 1961.

Tito had his own ideas about how to apply communism in Yugoslavia. Within three years after the end of the war, the Yugoslav Party had been read out of the Communist church. The satellite world began bubbling with heretical noises about "independent" communism, and the Russians cracked down on all satellite leaders who were not safe Stalinists. Stalin threatened Yugoslavia with military invasion, which was not carried out, and with economic sanctions, which were.

Enver Hoxha, head of the Albanian Communists, apparently was convinced that Marshal Tito looked upon Albania as his own satellite. So Albania stuck to Russia for protection against Yugoslavia until Khrushchev made a flamboyant effort to patch things up with Tito and launched his sensational program of de-Stalinization. The proposed reconciliation between Russia and Yugoslavia did not work out. But this and the posthumous disgrace of Hoxha's mentor, Stalin, scared Albania enough to seek the protective wing of Communist China—geographically remote but ideologically closer to Tirana than to Moscow. This is why, in early 1962, there were two rival Communist neighbors in Eastern Europe, one of them independent, one dependent on China, and neither a member of the Soviet bloc. But communism had come to power in both through military force during wartime occupation and in the absence of normal governmental controls. Communism gained power through the use of power, and kept it the same way.

How Communism Spread to China

In 1949 China became the world's largest Communist state. A dozen years later the United States had no official representative in Communist China. Not a single American newspaper correspondent was reporting from Peking. And the whole subject of Red China was still so emotionally and politically loaded as to preclude rational public discussion of the issues posed for United States foreign policy.

But the question is, How did the Chinese Communists happen to get control of China? The record is clear on important points that respond to the question.

For one thing, the Chinese Communist movement developed independently, without significant support or sponsorship from the Russian Party. Mao Tse-tung, of course, was a youthful disciple of Karl Marx, whose writings he discovered as a student in the library of the Middle School at Changsha. Over the years the Chinese Communists belonged to the Comintern, attended international Communist meetings, and ritually proclaimed their unbreakable solidarity with all the other Communist parties and their undying devotion to the Russian Party as the fountainhead of world communism.

But all was not smooth. Ideological fights within the Chinese Party and between the Chinese and Russian parties were recurrent affairs. Mao, who was one of the original founders of the Chinese Party and who established the first Communist provincial government in southern China in the late 1920s, was excommunicated for several years from the Central Committee of the Chinese Party. This insistence upon organizing the Chinese revolution around the rural peasants instead of the urban proletariat was pure heresy to the Russian Party.

It is clear that Stalin had little use for the Chinese Communists. He maintained normal relations with the Nationalist Government and gave every indication, including a postwar treaty with Chiang Kai-shek, of maintaining that relationship. It was not until 1945 that the Russians did a substantial favor for the Chinese Communists. In withdrawing from Manchuria after the defeat of Japan, Russian troops conveniently abandoned large stocks of captured Japanese war equipment, which were taken over by the Communists. It was a help. But it was late in the day and the help was not decisive. In any event there is nothing in the record of the long struggle for power in China that reflects any credit on the Russian masters of conflict management. It was a matter of Chinese versus Chinese.

For another thing, the record of China includes extensive documentation to support the conclusion that by 1943 or so the Nationalist revolution begun by Sun Yat-sen had lost its dynamic. The Kuomintang Party of Chiang Kai-shek had lost its popularity and the Nationalist government could not control the countryside. Chiang Kai-shek was unable to curb a deeply corrupted bureaucracy and the latter had lost control of the economy, which was in the throes of chaotic inflation. And the Nationalist armies were no longer willing to fight.

The reasons for all this are in controversy. But it is fact that the Nationalist government failed where every other government before it and since has failed: it could not provide enough food for a population which doubled in the course of the eighteenth and nineteenth centuries. It is fact that when the collapse came, there had been intermittent civil war in China between the Nationalists and the Communists for two decades. It is fact that undeclared war between China and Japan had been going on for eighteen years. And it is fact that both the Nationalists and the Communists devoted greater energies to the civil war between them than to the national war against Japan. Perhaps starvation, corruption, and twenty years of concurrent civil and international war are enough to explain the disintegration of a state. In any event that much is on the record.

The record also confirms that Mao controlled a trained, disciplined army of over 1,000,000 men. It was well equipped, and an unknown but substantial amount of the equipment was American-made. It had been captured from Nationalist troops or mysteriously diverted to the Communists without ever being used by the Nationalists. But for all its size, training, and equipment, the Communist armies did not have to win major military victories. The end came when Chiang, against the warnings of United States military advisers, dispatched his forces to overextended positions, where they simply fell to pieces without serious military engagement.

Perhaps the morale of Mao's troops was sustained by communist ideology. Perhaps Communist techniques of propaganda and infiltration were helpful to the Communist forces. Certainly their training in guerrilla warfare, including the administration of captured areas, was a factor in the Communist victory.

But behind all this was the material reality of military power: guns in the hands of Chinese Communists who were able and willing to use them. When the story of the Chinese Communist revolution can be seen in perspective, Mao's non-Marxist thesis may be given a central place in the plot: "Political power flows out of the barrel of a gun."

But even now we know that communism came to China as an indigenous movement without substantial outside help; the condition of its success was internal breakdown of the machinery of the Chinese state; and the decisive method of success was military conquest.

How Communism Spread Elsewhere

Since the end of World War II, Communism has come to power in assorted other places: North Korea, North Viet-Nam, Tibet, and Cuba.

In the case of North Korea, Communism was installed by the Red Army, which occupied the northern half of the country as part of the Allied plan for the conquest of Japan. It was an even easier affair than the analogous process in Eastern Europe. Two generations of Japanese rule and exploitation had left a political and cultural vacuum and a heritage of foreign control. The Red Army arrived with certain native Koreans, trained in Moscow during the war, serving as officers of Soviet troops. Among them was a Korean who, after a career as a bandit leader in Manchuria, had made his way to the Soviet Union. He assumed the name of a Korean national hero, Kim Il Sung, and it was he whom the Russians put in charge of the so-called Korean government. When everything was in order, Russian troops withdrew, leaving the Soviet Embassy to continue in the role of occupation authority.

It was as simple as that, though it is worth noting in passing that a handful of Korean Communists who had been trained in China were shunted by the Russians to unimportant jobs far from the seats of power.

In the case of Viet-Nam, guerrilla forces led by Communists, with the help of manpower, equipment, and training from China, were able to prevent the French from reimposing colonial rule in Indo-China when the Japanese withdrew their occupation forces. Again, there was no independent political force to oppose them. The opposition was from foreigners trying to restore colonial rule.

Thus Ho Chi Minh's Communist guerrillas could wrap themselves in the mantle of nationalism, of anticolonialism, of liberation, of independence. They could also fight in the jungles and paddies, raiding by night and gone by daylight, until after seven years of hit-and-run tactics they could bring heavy forces to the siege of the isolated fortress at Dien Bien Phu. By 1954 the French government of Pierre Mendès-

France was eager to end the long laceration of French forces, ready to settle at Geneva for Laos, Cambodia, and half of Viet-Nam as the independent but shaky successors to French Indo-China. At the beginning of 1962 Viet-Nam and Laos looked like the most vulnerable spots in the world to the relatively new Communist technique of "internal war."

The cause of Tibet was more like that of the Hungarian insurrection. Tibet had long been under some form of Chinese "suzerainty," but had been allowed substantial autonomy. After the Chinese Communists chased Chiang Kai-shek to Taiwan, they dispatched an army to help out with a program of "reform" to be prepared under the nominal chairmanship of the Dalai Llama. But the Tibetans did not cotton to Chinese plans for Tibet. The "reforms" were postponed.

Then, in 1959, tribesmen in the south opened a revolt. There were demonstrations in the capital of Lhasa. So the world's largest army invaded a small theocracy without regular armed forces, put down the revolt, and established military rule in the name of communism. There was no likelihood of serious opposition from the Tibetans or anyone else, though the event was a blow to Asian opinion of Communist China. As an Indian journalist put it to an American audience at the time: "Tibet did for us what Czechoslovakia did for you."

Then there is the prickly subject of Cuba and Castro. To say that the record is confused and confusing is to put it mildly. Yet some nuggets of fact can be discovered in the story.

It is fact that the Castro revolution presented itself to the Cuban people as a liberal, democratic movement to overthrow a corrupt dictatorship, to reinstate the Cuban Constitution, and to hold free elections. It is fact that this prospect was welcomed widely by the people of Cuba. While Castro led peasant guerrillas in the rural mountainside, his main support came from the middle classes in Havana. His victory was made possible, without serious military engagement, by the collapse of support for the Batista government. His assumption of power, which he said he did not want, was generally acclaimed in the Western Hemisphere as the dawn of a bright new day in the Caribbean.

It is fact that Castro said and reiterated that his movement was not Communist. But it is also fact that Castro soon appeared anxious to leap into the arms of Nikita Khrushchev and that some two years after the end of the revolution he said that Cuba was "one of the socialist states." On December 2, 1961, it was reported that Castro said that *after* the victory of the revolution he had become a "Marxist-Leninist," and on December 21 it was reported he said that he had been a Marxist-Leninist from the beginning of the revolution but had "called it something else" to insure success and to present ideas "which people were able to easily understand." The record does not show at which point Castro was lying—at which point a revolution which to most people had all the earmarks of a genuine, indigenous Cuban revolution against reactionary dictatorship became the creature of Cuban Communists and the vehicle of a new dictatorship.

Thus the Cuban case does not fit the pattern of conditions or techniques under which communism gained control of other areas. Nor is it clear where Cuba fits in the "Communist world," if at all. Castro made strenuous efforts to cuddle up to the Russians. The Russians made the most of it for propaganda purposes, but ducked flat commitments. And Castro's appetite for guerrilla fighting in rural areas fits the Chinese tradition better than the Russian.

Meanwhile the story of Cuba is muddied by the catastrophic invasion in the spring of 1961 by Cuban refugees with American support. By this time the enthusiasm for Castro in Latin America was on the wane, but the invasion fiasco in the Bay of Pigs revived his stock for a while by equating Fidelismo with "nonintervention."

By the end of 1961, however, Castro was again displaying the typical Communist talent for self-ostracism. Thirteen of the Western Hemisphere nations had broken diplomatic relations with Cuba and the operations of the Cuban propaganda offices of *La Prensa Libre* were being banned or circumscribed in Latin America. It was an open question whether the presence of a Communist revolutionary center "ninety miles from our shores" would strengthen Communist parties in Latin America or whether close association with a Communist-led police state would stir Latin America to look to its internal security—and to its appalling poverty.

The significant part of the record of communism in Cuba is yet to be written—as significant parts of how it happened are yet to be discovered.

"Land and Converts"

We are often reminded that since 1917 Communist parties have gained control of nations which together comprise one-quarter of the land surface of the earth. But has the "communist movement," as has been suggested, gained "converts at a faster rate than any political or religious movement in history?"

In 1948 the Communist Party won an election in San Marino; in 1960 it was voted out of office. In 1957 the Communist Party won an election in the Indian state of Kerala. By 1959 the Communists had made such a mess of things and inspired such popular resentment that the Indian government had no qualms about invoking an emergency provision of the Constitution to throw them out.

Everywhere else in all the world, Communist parties have failed to win the support of a majority of the voters in any national or state election. During the decade of the 1950s the fortunes of Communist parties fluctuated from time to time and place to place, but their prospects in Western Europe are now close to zero, and the general pattern in other areas is one of internal dissension and of organizational and financial problems. They have lost strength in more places than they have gained it.

This should not be surprising, for revolutionary communism is stuck with a dilemma: to gain the support of workers, the Communists must fight for better working conditions; but if working conditions improve, the excuse for revolution disappears and support of Communism falls off. Thus Communist parties have rough sledding in any progressive society: they must agitate for reform to earn support, but if reform is granted, they lose the support.

As for the devotion to communism in the countries controlled by Communist parties, the record is largely hidden. Some observers have suggested that Nikita Khrushchev could be elected in a free vote as President of the Soviet Union, though it is difficult to predict how people would behave in their first election. And though everyone is entitled to his hunch, it is impossible to know what the Chinese people think of their Communist masters. But it is not so difficult to deduce what the inhabitants of Eastern Europe think of the system. Riots in Germany and Poland and an insurrection in Hungary; millions of refugees and hundreds of miles of barbed wire, land mines, sentry towers, and police dogs; a concrete wall through the middle of a city to keep people on the Communist side—this is evidence enough. Popularity is not among the assets of communism. As United States Justice William O. Douglas put it, the Communists remain as "miserable merchants of unwanted goods." The Soviet Union has won the enmity of its wartime allies, which asked for nothing but friendly relations. Red China has managed to disaffect Asian leaders who desperately tried to get along with it. Neither Khrushchev nor Mao has a single reliable ally in the world. And Castro seems well on his way toward self-banishment from respectable international society.

The record examined in the previous chapter showed that the most fanatic of the converts to communism struggle for power among themselves, within Communist states and between Communist states. Combined with the story of how communism actually came to power over one-third of the world's population, the record now shows:

—*That Communism came to power in Russia by overnight* coup d'état *at the height of the catastrophe and chaos of World War I.*

—*That Communism came to power in Yugoslavia, Albania, and China in the aftermath of World War II by the application of superior military force controlled by national Communists.*

—*That Communism came to power in Latvia, Lithuania, Estonia, and Tibet through the military occupation of very weak states by very powerful states.*

—*That with some qualification for Czechoslovakia, Communism came to power in Eastern and Central Europe and in North Korea in the wake of World War II by the act of Soviet occupation authorities on the spot, backed up by overwhelming military force in place or readily available.*

—*That Communism came to North Viet-Nam in the wake of World War II and in the name of anticolonialism.*

—*That in most of these cases the country in question was seriously dislocated by war, civil war, occupation or some combination of these; in most cases there was no effective governmental control and no strong political alternative; and except for Indo-China in no case was there any serious likelihood of armed opposition from any big power.*

With the exception of Cuba, this is how the "Communist world" was built—only to subdivide later on. The record shows that the Communist world is not "monolithic" and that much of it was created out of chaos and disintegration. Otherwise it spread mainly by the application of superior power employed under safe circumstances. Neither ideology, propaganda, infiltration, subversion, or any of the dreaded weapons of Communist conquest have played a decisive role in the growth of Communist power. Communism has never been installed through free choice and has never triumphed over the effective opposition of the non-Communist forces of a national society.

In short, the record shows that the United States is not yet "encircled" by Communism.

The Arena of Cold War

The postwar stage has been dominated by the two pre-eminently superpowers. But their cold war contest is not conducted in a global vacuum. Other powers exist. Other forces are at work. And, appearances not withstanding, conflict has not monopolized world affairs since the end of World War II.

Beneath the clamor of cold war—parallel with the arms race, indifferent to the bipower concept of power, and largely overlooked by the strategists of big-power conflict—towering trends have been reshaping the world.

The record of cold war and communism outlined in Part One and Part Two has been put down as though the United States and the Soviet Union really had the world pretty much to themselves. Part Three attempts to put the cold war in the context of the larger reality of contemporary world affairs.

PART THREE

THE LARGER REALITY

CHAPTER SEVEN

Mr. Churchill and Mr. Jefferson

Winston Churchill was in fine fettle as World War II neared its climax. But in a speech to an appreciative Tory audience in the national election of 1945, his sensitive feel for the sweep of history suddenly deserted him and yielded to political exigency.

"I have not become His Majesty's First Minister," Mr. Churchill said, "to preside over the liquidation of the British Empire."

Two months later the British electorate spared him the agony and perhaps at the same time spared his name for the bright halls of posterity.

For as World War I provided the cover for the Young Turks and others to plot the dismemberment of the Ottoman Empire, World War II was a smoke screen for those who waited and watched and plotted for independence in India and Burma and Ceylon and Malaya, in Indonesia and French Indo-China, in Egypt, Syria, and Lebanon, in North Africa and, finally, in the vast reaches of tropical Africa. The end of World War II brought the collapse not only of Fascist Italy and Nazi Germany and Imperial Japan, but of the Western colonial system as well. It was not only the end of a war, but of an era and a particular system of world order. Throughout the nineteenth and half of the twentieth century Britain and France and Holland and Belgium and Portugal maintained order in Southern and Southeastern Asia, in the Middle East and in Africa. They financed what there was in the way of economic development. They brought what there was of education and public health. They conducted most of the world's trade, and financed it and insured it and carried it in their merchant ships. These few nations of Western Europe were bankers and brokers and traders and policemen to most of the world.

It was assumed, naturally and almost universally, that their national power, their economic prosperity, even their future existence, rested squarely on their overseas possessions. Communists and conservatives were as one on the point.

But at the end of the war, the jig was up. The European system of trade empires became a political anachronism. Pent-up demands for independence in the colonies, together with political realism, good conscience, and postwar weakness in Britain combined to unleash a tide of national liberation which, in the longer pull, may be given greater historical weight than the cold war itself.

When the Labour party came into power in Britain in 1945, Clement Atlee and Ernest Bevin presided over the start of the liquidation of His Majesty's Empire with dispatch and magnanimity, and at what service to the world we can only surmise.

If Britain was the symbol of one end of the European empire system, India was the symbol of the other. History therefore will take special note of an event which took place at the stroke of midnight, August 15, 1947, at Government House in New Delhi. On that occasion Jawaharlal Nehru —first son of a well-to-do lawyer, and himself a lawyer, Oxford-educated, a disciple of Mahatma Gandhi, three times jailed by the British for agitation, and now India's first prime minister—rose to observe the birth of a free and independent nation. India, which had known the invading armies of Darius in the fifth century before Christ and of Alexander in the third century, which had been milked by the Portuguese and the French and the English for centuries—India which had produced riches for others was now free to do what she could for her 400,000,000 people.

There were to be desperate days and frustrating years ahead for India. But on August 15, 1947, the former jewel of the British Empire became the world's largest democracy. An irreversible parade of decolonization took its first giant step. And the British Commonwealth of Nations began an astonishing transformation into a multiracial association of states. In 1945 the Commonwealth was composed of five nations with a combined population of about 95,000,000. By late 1961 there were twelve members with a combined population of some 620,000,000 people—more than 85 per cent of them Asians and Africans of the former colonies.

In the decade and a half following India's independence, while the cold war was grabbing most of the headlines, over forty new nations were born out of the death of the Western empire. Some arrived painlessly; some by a kind of Caesarean section; and some, in deep travail. All were eligible, big powers willing, for membership in the United Nations. All were free to be heard for the first time in world forums.

Some 900,000,000 people live in the places that became nations between 1945 and 1961—more than one-fourth of all the people in the world, about one-half of the total population of the non-Communist world. Thus while nine formerly independent countries were transferred to Communist domination, forty odd countries were released from Western domination. While 700,000,000 Chinese and some 125,000,-000 others, few of whom had ever lived under democracy, were subjected to Communist totalitarianism, 900,000,000 got a chance to try freedom.

The drive for statehood, of course, was not new. In previous centuries it created the nation-states of Britain and France, then of Germany and Italy. At the close of World War I it broke up the Austro-Hungarian and the Ottoman empires.

What was new was that nationalism was no longer a Western phenomenon; it had burst into flame in the sleeping societies of Asia and Africa that had been stagnant for centuries, and where a large part of mankind happens to live.

Nationalism, often violent, convulsive, formless, was committed to one thing: independence. It fought under the banner of anticolonialism. It often became anti-Western and sometimes anti-white. It could whip mobs into emotional frenzies and irrational violence. It was, as one Asian leader said, an "antifeeling"—no substitute for a positive political philosophy. But as another Asian put it: "You might just as well try to stop steam."

In the end nationalism turned out to be the most powerful political force of the mid-twentieth century, a force capable of pulling down the European empires, capable of mobilizing discordant societies for common action, capable of winning concessions from much stronger states, and capable of giving a very hard time to an elaborate Communist conspiracy to capture and subvert it.

But when national independence is won, the foreign enemy disappears, the battle cry fades, the common cause which united everyone in common action is no more. For the first time the revolution needs a domestic program.

And independence alone fills no hungry bellies. By itself it does nothing to substitute clean water for polluted water;

nothing to cure malaria or trachoma or bilharziasis; nothing to reduce infant mortality, or to teach children to write, or make fallow soil fertile, or train men to make steel or run businesses or hospitals or railroads or government agencies. Unless independence is followed by signs of progress, victory turns sour. Unless nationalist leaders can deliver something beyond liberation, they may slip into political repression at home to silence the critics, or into foreign adventure to divert attention from domestic failure.

The hurricane winds of nationalism that blew down empires to leave nations in their wake in the mid-twentieth century brought independence to nearly a billion people with average incomes of less than $200 a year, with life expectancy of less than forty years, with the odds against their ever learning to read and write. But those who were educated had been exposed to the wonders of industrialism, and to the records of material progress in the West and in Russia as well. For the first time they knew they were poor and they knew that their poverty was not ordained by fate. The result was a new clamor for a better material shake out of life, a phenomenon which has come to be called the revolution of rising expectations. Barbara Ward has called this revolution, together with revolution of nationalism, the "twin furies of the twentieth century."

So nationalist revolutions, once successful, must turn inward to deal with popular hopes for more decent standards of living.

It may well be that out in the far byways of the world people know little about the power struggle among the major nations and care less about the "battle for the mind of man." Like backwoodsmen everywhere, they are suspicious of city slickers who want to change their way of life. But whether or not the revolution of rising expectations has rippled the surface of human complacency in the last Asian or African village, the new leaders, one and all, have staked their political careers on ending the reign of poverty. They know, or at least believe, that they cannot survive unless they produce on their promises.

Mr. Jefferson's Prophesies

The "twin furies" of the twentieth century owe nothing whatever to communism. The ideology, the agitation, and the subversive propaganda which fed the revolutions of national independence and rising expectations came out of the Western Age of Enlightenment. The original agents of today's turmoil were the political ideas and the scientific advances of Europeans and Americans. The culprits responsible for the vast upheavals of the mid-twentieth century include such names as Tom Paine and Tom Jefferson, Henry Ford and Thomas Alva Edison.

It was the Declaration of Independence, not the *Communist Manifesto,* which laid down the doctrine for the independence movement that raced through the Middle East and Asia and into Africa in the decade and a half following World War II.

> . . . We hold these truths to be self-evident, that all men are created equal, that they are endowed by their Creator with certain unalienable Rights, that among these are Life, Liberty and

> the pursuit of Happiness. That to secure these rights, Governments are instituted among Men, deriving their just powers from the consent of the governed, That whenever any Form of Government becomes destructive of these ends, it is the Right of the People to alter or to abolish it, and to institute new Government, laying its foundation on such principles and organizing its powers in such form, as to them shall seem most likely to effect their Safety and Happiness. . . .

This was the doctrine that fueled the fires of Asian, Arab, and African nationalism. This was the document that was studied and revered by the revolutionaries and resistance leaders. These were the words that were paraphrased in the declarations and the preambles to constitutions in new nation after new nation.

When President Achmed Sukarno of Indonesia opened the Bandung Conference of Asian and African nations in 1955, he quoted from the "Midnight Ride of Paul Revere," not *Das Kapital.* When Prime Minister U Nu of Burma described his nation's foreign policy before a joint session of the Senate and House in Washington the same year, he traced its policies to George Washington, not Nikolai Lenin. When President Nasser was justifying his seizure of the Suez Canal to an American diplomat in 1956, he quoted the authority of Thomas Jefferson, not Mao Tse-tung.

And what came to pass in the mid-twentieth century was predicted in the early days of the American Revolution. Tom Paine had said of the Revolution: "America made a stand, not for herself only, but for the world. . . ."

And Jefferson wrote of the Declaration of Independence in his last public letter: "May it be to the world what I believe it will be . . . the signal for arousing men to burst the chains under which monkish ignorance and superstition had persuaded them to bind themselves, and to assume the blessings and security of self-government. . . ."

To the nationalist revolutionaries and leaders of Asia, Africa and the Middle East:

—*The "unalienable rights" of men proved more appealing than the "iron laws of history."*

—*"Life, Liberty and the pursuit of Happiness" were more attractive than class warfare.*

—*The "Right of the people . . . to institute new Government" was sounder doctrine than the revolution of the proletariat.*

—*And to lay the foundation of governments "on such principles . . . as to them seem most likely to effect their Safety and Happiness" seemed better policy than "international solidarity."*

In the end, the Declaration of Independence proved more revolutionary than the *Communist Manifesto*. The ideas of Jefferson were more subversive than those of Karl Marx, and he was a much better prophet to boot.

It is a long way from Massachusetts to Malagasay, but the shot first heard at Concord ricocheted at last to the ends of the earth in the mid-twentieth century.

The other "fury" of the mid-twentieth century, the revolutionary demand for a better standard of living, was also foreseen by Thomas Jefferson. The same letter quoted above contained this insight: "The general spread of the light of science has already laid open to every view the palpable truth, that the mass of mankind has not been born with saddles on their backs, nor a favored few booted and spurred, ready to ride them. . . ."

This "palpable truth" to Jefferson did not become evident to "every view" for a long time. But halfway through the twentieth century his comment about the "light of science," like his prediction of the impact of the American Revolution, was vindicated.

In Jefferson's time the "light of science" was about to produce the technology for an industrial revolution which began, of course, in England and Europe. But it was in America that the first mass-consumption society began to take shape, thanks to a fortuitous combination of factors. These factors included immense natural resources, a continental free-trade area, a small population and consequent shortage of labor; "foreign aid" in the form of investments and loans from abroad; "technical assistance" in the form of immigrant skills; and the gradual reform of the capitalist system.

Close behind the industrial revolution came the power revolution: electrification of factories, offices, houses, farms.

And the revolution in transport: railroads, automobiles, highways, aircraft, jets.

And the revolution in agricultural technology, seemingly advanced but perhaps even now still in the threshold stage.

And the revolution in communications: high-speed presses; the telegraph; the telephone; motion pictures that first flickered and then talked; still photographs transmitted by wire; then moving pictures transmitted by TV. All these appeared in quick order, until a man could sit in his living room by the Golden Gate and watch Nikita Khrushchev offer "full and complete disarmament" to delegates from almost every country in the world at the United Nations General Assembly, hard by the East River in Manhattan.

By this time the United States population as a whole had to deal with the problem of what to do with its disposable income after meeting basic needs for food, clothing, and shelter. This simply had never happened before. But it had exposed to "every view" Jefferson's "palpable truth" that "mankind has not been born with saddles on their backs." And in 1958 it prompted historian Arnold Toynbee to write:

> Our age will be remembered not for its horrifying crimes or its astonishing inventions but because it is the first generation since the dawn of history in which mankind dared to believe it is practical to make the benefits of civilization available to the whole human race.

Yet the modern explosion of science and technology is only beginning, for the biggest change of all is the change in the rate of change. It has been estimated that more progress has been made in science in the past fifty years than in all preceding history; that about 90 per cent of all the scientists who ever lived are alive today; that the sum total of scientific knowledge is doubling about every nine years; that in some fields whole new technologies can be expected to emerge every three or four years.

In 1959 J. Robert Oppenheimer looked about him and concluded that ". . . in this immense, almost thundering impact of discovery upon tradition we have come to a new phase of human history."

Revolutionary nationalism, which brought independence

to forty-odd nations and 900,000,000 people; a new crusade against the poverty of half the people of the non-Communist world; technological revolutions in industry, agriculture, power, transport, and communications: these were part of the larger reality of world affairs as the giants were preoccupied with cold war.

CHAPTER EIGHT

The United States and Russia Meet the Furies

In classical communist doctrine, nationalism is a contemptible bourgeois invention. But this did not prevent the Communist Stalin from leading a "great patriotic war" in defense of the "fatherland." Nor did it prevent the Communist Khrushchev from becoming the personal champion of national independence and full sovereignty once it became the magic rallying cry throughout Asia, the Middle East, and Africa.

From 1955 onward the First Secretary of the Communist Party of the U.S.S.R. picked up where Woodrow Wilson left off as the chief sponsor of the doctrine of self-determination.

And Soviet delegates to the United Nations became more anticolonial than the anticolonialists. At the General Assembly meeting in 1961, for example, the Soviet Delegation fought hard for a Soviet resolution proposing that all remaining dependencies be granted unconditional independence by 1962. Not even the new African members would vote for it.

For Russia, the collapse of the European empires presented no policy problem at all.

It was made to order for propaganda themes and slogans. Down with imperialism! Freedom for everybody—now! Self-determination for all!

It also offered a chance to identify the Soviet Union, if not communism itself, with the deepest urge and most potent political force of the times.

And if some of the new nations gaining independence happen to be economically nonviable, tribally split, and politically inexperienced, so much the better from the Russian point of view. The record shows that political chaos and the absence of effective national institutions are the happiest conditions for Communist maneuver.

Best of all, the "colonial issue" seemed to offer to the Soviet Union the sharpest wedge in sight for splitting the United States from its European friends and allies. Which is exactly why the United States was over the barrel on the "colonial issue."

American Dilemma

Most Americans instinctively side with those who raise the banner of freedom; their sympathies go out to all who would be rid of foreign domination; they react positively to the symbol of "self-determination."

And yet during the 1950s the United States government could never quite come to terms with the prairie fires of nationalism sweeping through Asia, the Middle East, Africa and, in special form, Latin America.

For one thing, United States attention tended to be focused so hard on the crisis spots around the Sino-Soviet periphery—on the imperatives of military defense—that the swirling affairs of the "third world" seemed remote and irrelevant distractions from the main show in the big tent of the bipolar world.

For another thing, the new nations, having rid themselves of dependence on one set of big powers were not looking for new attachments to other big powers. They wanted no part of the cold war and declared their "neutrality" in what seemed to them a private fight between superpowers. For a while the United States government seemed to believe that anyone unwilling to line up on "our side" was necessarily in the other camp, and did little to search for common ground with the new nations.

Finally, the proprietors of the remaining European empires happened to be our natural friends and military allies in NATO.

If the United States sided squarely with its European friends on colonial issues, it would be at one with the "imperialists," and at odds with the rising young nations. If the United States went all out for the anticolonial cause, it might endanger the Atlantic alliance. It was damned-if-you-do and damned-if-you-don't.

For years the United States vacillated uncomfortably in the middle—advising the Europeans to make concessions sooner rather than later, advising the nationalists to be patient and reasonable. Except when the United States sided with Egypt and the Soviet Union against Britain and France in the Suez affair, United States performance on the "colonial" issue was not fully pleasing either to the Europeans or the break-away colonies.

Then, in 1961, a foreboding silence in Portuguese Africa was broken by news of the predictable rebellion in Angola. In this sealed-off colony, which the Portuguese claimed to be an integral part of Portugal, Africans and Europeans were slaughtering each other. When the matter came up in the United Nations, the United States stepped out of the middle position to vote for a resolution calling on Portugal to stop bloodshed and start reform in Angola. With Britain and France abstaining, the United States voted against a military ally whose bases and other installations were considered important strategic assets by her military establishments.

The United States finally had decided to pay the price of lining up with the future in Africa, and with its own past. It was only a few months later that the United States was in the middle again between its French ally and its Tunisian friend in a dispute, accompanied by violence, over the French naval base at Bizerte. But the United States voted for a resolution calling for a pull-back of French forces and the start of negotiations, to the undisguised displeasure of General de Gaulle. And at the General Assembly in 1961 the United States supported a resolution calling for the ultimate end of the remnants of colonialism everywhere.

Nobody thought the clean-up process would be easy. For what remained on the agenda were the hard-core cases plus a few score islands and enclaves which could never be defined as "nations." But by the end of 1961 the colonial issue was beginning to run out of gas. And the "'anti-imperialist" theme song of Soviet propaganda was being played back to its composers. In September 1961 President Kennedy told the General Assembly that "the tide of self-determination has not yet reached the Communist empire. . . ." In November, Ambassador Adlai Stevenson had circulated to all United Nations members a memorandum documenting the Soviet Union's "own record of imperialist oppression and exploitation," a record of "the largest colonial empire which has ever existed in all history."

The Soviet "Economic Offensive"

Mr. Khrushchev did his best to get aboard the nationalist revolutions during the demise of the European empires. He also tried to line up with the revolution of rising expectations.

Beginning in about 1955 the Soviet Union, which has little or no theoretical use for world trade, opened a program of aid, trade, and credits for selected countries in Asia, Africa, and the Middle East. In the United States, Soviet trade was likely to be seen as "Communist tentacles"; Soviet technicians even more surely were "agents" who were "infiltrating" the victim country and preparing it for "subversion"; and nations accepting Soviet aid were said to be "down the drain," and "lost" to the free world.

Mr. Khrushchev has been forthright on the point that the Russian government was more interested in the political than the economic results of aid-trade programs. But the record does not justify the early alarm at Russia's emergence from the cocoon of economic isolationism. Nor does it make clear the political impact of economic operations which a military wall could not "contain."

In operation, the Soviet aid-trade system had a number of assets when compared with the United States "foreign aid" program.

Soviet assistance frequently went to the projects dearest to the hearts of the leaders of the developing countries: military arms and the High Aswan Dam in Egypt; paved streets and a modern bakery for the capital of Afghanistan; a steel mill for India; a hospital and sports stadium for Burma. In contrast, United States–financed projects tended to have less "impact value": aid for a rural extension service or agricultural research station, training in public administration, devising the curriculum for a medical school, and such useful but undramatic ventures.

Soviet assistance took into account the symbolic importance of industrial projects for countries determined to modernize in a hurry. In contrast, United States officials tended to prefer "first things first," and were allergic to showy projects susceptible to the allegation that they are "economic monuments."

Soviet assistance involved no visible "interference" in the affairs of the other country, no economic analysis, no engineering surveys, no mission of Russians to supervise the aid and insist upon auditing its use. In contrast, the United States aid administration was accountable to Congress for detailed justification and reporting and for supervision on the spot.

Soviet assistance can be brought to bear quickly. When French technicians pulled out of Guinea en masse, Soviet technicians were at work within the week. In contrast, the American aid machinery is likely to grind for eighteen months between a request for assistance and a project start.

Soviet assistance usually is granted on attractive terms: loans at 2 or 2.5 per cent with repayment in commodities, including some commodities in burdensome surplus for the other country. In contrast, United States loans, until 1961, were normally at 4 per cent interest. And the United States was unable to figure out how to relieve other countries of surplus stocks. For one thing, the surplus was, by definition, what was left over after other countries, including the United States, had bought what they were able and willing to buy.

By and large the Russians appeared to do well in propagandizing their aid-trade program. Nothing terribly clever about it; they simply get the best mileage they can by such simple devices as announcing each deal several times, first when it is agreed to reach an agreement, again when the agreement is reached, and once more when the agreement goes into effect.

In the five years after 1955 the Soviet aid-trade program reached substantial proportions, a total of some $5,000,000,000 worth. But much of this was for credits to be drawn on over a period of years, and it looked much larger than it was because it had never been done before at all. Trade between some of the developing countries and the Soviet "bloc" was on the rise, but from a very low base.

American critics, especially the most fervent anti-Communists, seem to take it for granted that the Soviet aid-trade performance has been flawless. The record does not bear them out. There were not infrequent delays in the delivery of Soviet goods and there were complaints about the quality of some Soviet products delivered under aid-trade agreements. Some Russian technicians displayed an obtuse inability to understand the language or the strange ways of their host countries and had to be sent home. And there were some first-rate failures and plain goofs, like unloading cement on the docks of Rangoon and leaving it there until the rains set in, setting the cement in the process. Equivalent American blunders touch off Congressional investigations, inspire "exposés" in some quarters of the press, and lead the *Wall Street Journal* to conclude again that the entire aid program should be stopped cold while the whole matter is carefully restudied.

What's more, the acceptance by the Soviet Union of surplus commodities was not always an unmitigated blessing for the other countries. In several cases the Soviets resold the commodities in third countries at cut-rate prices, thus fouling that market for the country from which they took the goods in the first place. This happened in the case of Burmese rice and Egyptian cotton, to the considerable distress of the Burmese and the Egyptians.

Some Americans became particularly alarmed by a special aspect of Soviet "economic warfare," the sudden sale of large quantities of Russian surpluses on world markets. But this seemed to be something less than a major effort to disrupt world markets. In retrospect the "dumping" of Soviet aluminum in 1959 looks more like a clumsy effort to get rid of temporary overproduction than a serious effort to break world prices.

And in several instances such Soviet actions backfired. For example, when the Russians sold large quantities of tin at less than world prices, there were those who quickly saw through the Soviet strategy. It was to further depress the economy of Bolivia, which depends inordinately on the export of tin, throwing Bolivian tin miners out of work, and strengthening the hands of the Communists within the Bolivian trade unions.

Perhaps that was the purpose; no one outside can know. But the result was angry protests to Moscow from Malaya and Indonesia, which also export tin. Soviet authorities quietly agreed not to do this again, and accepted a voluntary quota suggested by the International Tin Committee. If their purpose was disruptive, they found out the hard way that in the intricate free world economy, pressure on country *X*, which they might want to harm, can simultaneously hurt countries *Y* and *Z*, which they might want to befriend.

In at least three cases the Soviet Union openly applied crude economic pressure for political gain or reprisal: Yugoslavia, Finland, and Albania. In the first two cases, the slack was taken up by other countries in the free world. In the case of Albania the Chinese Communists rushed to the rescue. If hidden pressures were applied against other countries, the record shows no evidence of Soviet success.

In the meantime the "tentacles" of trade and aid did not appear fatal. Colonel Nasser kept his local Communists in jail and Radio Cairo was not too subverted to be unable to carry on a propaganda slugging match with Radio Moscow. Iraq miraculously stayed out of the Communist camp despite extreme dependence on Soviet assistance. Burma sent home a group of Soviet technicians who made themselves unwelcome. And in late December 1961, President Sékou Touré of Guinea said that he had broken up a "clandestine group" of "Marxist-Leninists" with ties to Moscow. The Russian ambassador departed for home, and Vice-Premier Mikoyan flew off to Guinea to see what he could do to repair a relationship which had failed to prosper despite lavish financial and technical aid from the Soviet Union.

The unanswerable question remained: To what extent, if any, did Soviet aid help convince poverty-ridden countries that the Soviet system is the only fit vehicle for rapid modernization of poor countries and that the socialist system of production is superior to the capitalist system of production? This, after all, is what Khrushchev has said he is counting on to produce a Communist one world.

"Mutual Security"

Before Pearl Harbor the United States made mighty contributions to ultimate Allied victory with its Lend-Lease program of aid to Britain and the Soviet Union. The program was continued throughout the war, to help win it.

Immediately after the war, the United States was the major contributor to the huge United Nations Relief and Rehabilitation Agency. Its military occupation forces ran large-scale relief operations. Emergency loans were made to Britain, France, Italy, and Austria, and aid toward the recovery of former enemies was generous without historic precedent. All this was to help repair the damages of war.

The Truman Doctrine, though it stressed economic aid, was triggered by Soviet military pressure against Turkey and a going Communist insurrection in Greece.

And the Marshall Plan, however worthy of the tributes heaped upon it, was inspired, after all, by fear that Stalin's Russia might pluck all Europe from postwar chaos.

None of these massive and successful uses of United States resources abroad had any relation to the revolution of rising expectations. In 1949, however, President Truman took an initiative which he later said would be remembered in history as the most important act of his seven years in office. In his State of the Union message that year, Mr. Truman made the now-famous Point Four offer of technical assistance to help the less developed world build the foundations of modern economies.

The technical assistance program, as originally conceived, was to be followed by a program of loans for economic development projects. But policy differences within the Administration kept the lending aspect bottled up until the whole overseas aid enterprise was knocked off the tracks by the outbreak of the Korean War in 1950.

From that time on, at least until the late 1950s, there was little or no hesitancy about allocating resources for military aid to allies abroad. A Defense Support Program added economic grants to further sustain allies carrying inordinately heavy defense burdens. Other grants and loans were made to governments which seemed challenged by external or internal Communist pressures. Within this complex of "foreign aid" the technical assistance program grew steadily in scope and experience.

But from 1952 to 1960 all of them were lumped into one piece of legislation called the Mutual Security Act, bespeaking the defensive context in which both Congress and the Administration considered overseas aid. Economic assistance, which was less than military aid, went mostly to the hot spots on the Sino-Soviet periphery. The rest of it was justified in passing, on humanitarian and welfare grounds, but mainly in relation to the "Soviet economic offensive." Poverty, it was said repeatedly, should be attacked for other reasons, but mainly because it was a "breeding ground for communism." Even the United States contribution to the United Nations Children's Fund was appropriated under the Mutual Security Appropriations Act.

And the Congress insisted on reauthorizing the whole Mutual Security Program every year, and appropriating funds on a year-to-year basis as though it were dealing with some temporary crisis with an annoying habit of popping up again every twelve months.

In the meantime there were rumblings from the southern half of the Western Hemisphere. Twice President Eisenhower sent his brother on tours of Latin America, and twice he reported, first in bland language and then in notes of urgent alarm that Latin America had great and unfilled economic needs which threatened to explode politically. Nevertheless, in a series of conferences over the years, United States delegates spoke firmly of defending the Western Hemisphere from Communist encroachment, but lost interest when the question of United States help for economic development came up. Our delegates were always happy to have another committee appointed, but advised the Latin delegates to put their trust in private investment. When it came to the question of how to deal with fluctuating world prices for the export commodities on which Latin foreign earnings depend, the United States was not prepared to discuss the matter. Latin America seemed a long way from the Sino-Soviet periphery. Nonetheless:

In 1957, eight years after the Point Four proposals, the Congress established a Development Loan Fund to help finance on liberal terms the economic growth of less developed countries in Asia, Africa, and Latin America.

In 1954 the United States began a "surplus food disposal program" by selling and giving food to less developed countries from government-held surplus stocks.

In 1958 the United States took part in a major international effort to help India complete her second Five-Year Plan.

In 1959 the United States dropped its long opposition and agreed to help form an Inter-American Development Bank.

And in 1960 President Eisenhower announced an emergency program of direct United States aid for Latin America.

At that time, the United States was still the largest source of financial and technical assistance for the newly freed and newly awakened nations. But other industrialized countries were beginning to add substantial resources; international agencies were under way with their own programs of assistance; and private American organizations were getting deeper and deeper into the business of economic and social growth abroad.

The dimensions of their mutual task was suggested, if not defined, by a statistical comparison. During the decade of the 1950s, per capita annual income for 1,250,000,000 people, in a hundred less developed countries and territories, rose by approximately $10.00; in the United States the comparable figure was $550.

The cold war decade and a half between 1946 and 1960 appeared to many to overwhelm the affairs of the postwar world. But the old system of preserving order in the most populous areas of the world was coming apart simultaneously, and a parade of new nations were arising with insistent demands to be rid of their traditional poverty. Here is a summary of the record of these events, and the efforts of the superpowers to deal with them:

—*The empires collapsed but the home countries did not.*

—*Not one of the forty-odd new nations emerging from the break-up of European empires elected to establish a Communist state; the ideas of Thomas Jefferson proved more compelling than those of Karl Marx.*

—*The U.S.S.R.'s efforts to blow with the winds of the nationalist revolution proved useful for a while, but by 1961 the breeze was threatening to turn against her.*

—*After an uncomfortable period of being caught in the middle, the United States in 1961 came to terms with the anticolonial revolution without serious damage to the Western alliance.*

—*The Soviet aid-trade program had a potential political impact as evidence that communism offers rapid eco-*

nomic progress, but the "tentacles" of trade with Russia did not prove to be fatal.

—United States efforts to meet the revolution of rising expectations were substantial, but retarded and limited by a long fixation on military defense.

But another revolution, a quiet one, was adding still another dimension to contemporary affairs despite the cold war.

CHAPTER NINE

The Fitful Trend

In one sense, history is like the Hudson River: at certain times the tides are running in opposite directions simultaneously. And there never was a time when the ocean of history knew so many strong tides, some on the surface and some deeper down, as during the decade and a half following the end of World War II.

The surface tides were most noticeable: the surge of Communist expansion; the opposing surge of United States containment; the stormy course of nationalist revolution; the insistent flood of new demands for a modern standard of living.

But largely obscured by the fog of cold war, still another, and older, tide was on the loose again. It was the fitful trend which threads the story of history: the reluctant stages through which human society stumbles toward a world community. In the postwar years there was a new resurgence of this trend, a quiet tide which someday might carry the United States and the world at large into the clear, beyond the cold war.

But it was almost hidden from public view. World attention was too distracted by the thunder of conflict between the giant powers; world attention was too transfixed on their recurring crises; world emotion was too charged by the fear that someone would press the fatal button and bring to a violent end the whole civilizing process which someone has called "an interesting experiment of the higher anthropoids."

The story of this hidden revolution was written in bits and pieces which seldom were put together. It was the story of a new reaching out across national frontiers, of an unsure but insistent groping for new international arrangements, the sudden emergence of a new skyline of international institutions in a vague but discernible world community.

The story begins back with the Marshall Plan and with a stroke of genius or luck which inspired the organizational framework of the European Recovery Program. On the face of it, it is not an exciting story. But the end accomplishment of the Marshall Plan was not that it helped Europe recover from the damage of war, nor even that it probably saved Western Europe from communism. Its end accomplishment was that it started Europe on the road to unification.

The start of that road was a not-very-impressive piece of governmental machinery whose historic mission was to be performed under a dull name, the Organization for European Economic Cooperation, or OEEC. The OEEC was the unit established in Paris, at American insistence, to co-ordinate the recovery programs of the nations receiving United States aid. Dull or not, it is worthy of brief but respectful attention.

Prior to the Marshall Plan, the nations of Europe struggled to recover alone. Each spun out a web of restrictions against each other's goods and currencies; each tried to follow a nationalist path toward national recovery. None of them had any stomach at all for the international organization which the Americans asked them to establish.

But the United States was in an invulnerable position. In effect it told Britain and the European nations to draw up their own recovery programs, agree among themselves how the aid would be divided, and present a consolidated set of requirements.

There was no other way to get the American aid. So sixteen nations reluctantly set about the strange and distasteful business of working together for mutual recovery. As the delegates began to confront each other around conference tables at the Palais de Chaillot near the Bois de Boulogne in Paris, a phenomenon of the first water got under way: the British submitted their own recovery program to be reviewed, criticized, and revised by Italians, Greeks, Swedes, and others—and every other country did the same thing.

As it turned out, the experience was not as painful as everyone had expected. In fact, as the advantages emerged through the murk of nationalist tradition, they rather liked this new business. Within a short time the nations of Europe learned what one of their officials referred to later as the "habit of co-operation."

The OEEC before long established a European Payments Union to clear the international trading accounts of its members and the European Productivity Agency as a clearing house for technical information. Then the six nations of Western Europe established the European Coal and Steel Community to merge facilities and open a common market for these products. Then came EURATOM for common atomic energy facilities; then the Common Market of the European six, an economic community with an advisory legislative arm and a system of arbitration.

The nations which fought most of history's great wars were putting all that behind them. Europe was becoming the second greatest industrial complex in the world, serving a market the size of the United States. With rising incomes and rising demands, Spain and Turkey and Greece were brought into a special association with the other members of the Common Market. An economic renaissance was in the making. The United States was no longer unique as a mass-consumption society.

Through all this the United States was an interested witness, prodding more or less gently at each step. United States policy, starting with the Marshall Plan, had borne such healthy fruit that *U.S. News and World Report,* a consistent editorial opponent of "foreign aid," splashed on the cover of an issue in 1959: "The World's Biggest Success Story—Now It Can Be Told." When it was told on the inside pages, the world's biggest success story turned out to be the Marshall Plan and how it had led to the European Economic Community.

But the Common Market included only the six nations of Western Europe. In 1959 an attempt to bring in Britain, Scandinavia, Switzerland, and Austria failed. Britain then organized these countries into the European Free Trade Association, called the Outer Seven, and for several years the public prints were full of alarms and excursions about the "split" of Europe into "rival trade blocs."

Again, the United States was an interested spectator, and more. Under Secretary of State Douglas Dillon took some quiet soundings in Europe. The OEEC, he suggested, had outgrown some of its functions. Perhaps it was time to reorient its mission, especially in the direction of co-ordinating Western aid to the less developed world. Perhaps it was time for the United States and Canada, which had been associate members without a vote, to come in as full members of a refurbished organization.

A main point of the Dillon proposals, which was kept more or less in the background, was the idea that a reorganized OEEC might somehow manage to bring The Six and The Seven together. In the meantime, it would serve as a "forum" for co-ordinating the foreign economic policies of the leading Western powers, and a place where the major exporters of capital, including Japan, could co-ordinate their aid to the developing world.

The Europeans already had been discussing a new role for the OEEC. After some nervousness, the members agreed to the Dillon suggestions, and at the end of 1960 a treaty was initiated for the conversion of the OEEC into the OECD—Organization for Economic Cooperation and Development—with the United States and Canada as full members. *European* was out of the title; *development* was in. The next year the United States Senate and the other Parliaments agreed, and the OECD came into being.

The countries which had been aided by the Marshall Plan were now joined with the United States in an effort to work out fair shares and co-ordinated programing of aid for the world which emerged from the disintegration of their empires. And before long the nations of the OECD had set themselves a target for economic growth throughout the Atlantic area for the decade of the 1960s: a 50 per cent increase of combined national incomes. Thus the OECD sought to harmonize both the internal economic policies of its members and their external economic relations with the rest of the world.

Then, in the summer of 1961, after a year or more of anguished indecision, Britain took the plunge and applied for admission to the European Common Market. If negotiations work out, the other members of the Outer Seven said they would come in, too—though Nikita Khrushchev was putting the heat on Austria and the Scandinavian countries to stay out.

"Once Britain joins," said the *New York Journal of*

Commerce in mid-August, the next step might be to a "move toward some kind of North Atlantic common market, including the U.S. and Canada. . . ."

Thus Stalin's grab of Eastern Europe, his meddling in Western Europe, and his pressures in Germany after World War II did more than induce the containment policy and the birth of NATO. It set in motion a chain of events which led to the unification of Europe and its association with the United States and Canada in a new vision of an Atlantic Community. This could hardly have been Stalin's purpose. For the Atlantic Community includes over 400,000,000 of the most skilled and prosperous people in the world, with an industrial complex some four times more powerful than the combined industrial plant of the Communist world. In addition they possessed special links to the new British Commonwealth and the former French colonies in Africa.

On January 10, 1962, Walter Lippmann looked at the prospect of Atlantic Community and told the members of the Women's National Press Club:

> . . . I believe that in the months to come we shall engage ourselves in the long and complicated, but splendidly constructive, task of bringing together in one liberal and progressive economic community all the trading nations which do not belong to the Communist society.
>
> I dare to believe that this powerful Western economic community will be able to live safely and without fear in the same world as the Soviet Union, and the rising power and influence of the Western society will exert a beneficent magnetic attraction upon Eastern Europe. . . .

Mr. Lippmann's analysis would not be good news in the Kremlin.

Other New Communities

The reaching out across national frontiers was not limited to the European and Atlantic areas, nor was all in response to Soviet aggressiveness. In hesitant fits and starts, but all in the same direction, the tide toward free association in the non-Communist world ran strong in the postwar period.

The Organization of American States had political, economic, and public-health agencies, and a related investment bank, as the institutional foundation of a Western Hemisphere Community.

In Central America five nations, despite political feuding, stumbled toward a common market, common development and research institutions, common planning for industrialization. The Treaty of Economic Integration of Central America, signed in 1960, brought Nicaragua, Costa Rica, El Salvador, Guatemala, and Honduras into a commitment to build another economic community.

In South America, seven nations, including Brazil and Argentina, set up the Latin American Free Trade Association in early 1961, aimed at building a common market within a dozen years for the dominant part of the Latin American economy.

In Southeast Asia, the British Commonwealth in 1951 set up the Colombo Plan as a forum in which the nations of the area compare national development plans, swap technical assistance, plan regional development projects, and talk of some kind of a Southeast Asian common market of the future.

Even in Africa, where nationalism was used as a jimmy to pry new countries out of old empires, the nationalist leaders talked increasingly of regional and continental economic arrangements. Even as the Congo was being torn apart by provincial secession, most leaders of young Africa seemed to sense that economic nationalism belonged in the dead past with colonialism.

In the Far East, Japan converted recovery from war to an economic resurgence as remarkable as Europe's; in the late 1950s her industrial economy was growing faster than the Soviet Union's. Japan was beginning to lend capital and technical assistance to less prosperous nations in Southeast Asia. And by 1961 a regional center was established in Tokyo to serve as a clearinghouse for technical information for seventeen nations of Asia.

The Arab states were too torn by internal rivalries to do much about economic co-operation, but an Arab development bank was at least on paper.

Thus it was that during the 1950s and on into the 1960s economic nationalism was giving way to economic co-operation in the non-Communist world; national markets were merging into regional markets; national institutions were blending into regional institutions.

In 1959 Sir Oliver Franks put his finger on this trend and described economic regionalism as "a half-way house at a time when single nations are no longer viable and the world is not ready to become one."

New communities of nations were aborning, part of the larger political reality of a world distracted by the tempests of cold war.

"Man's Best Hope"

Another part of the larger reality was the United Nations. By early 1962 the United Nations had been glorified and damned, eulogized and discarded, hailed and buried more often than any institution in history. Every success was greeted as the opening of the millennium. Every failure was bemoaned as the dawn of doom. After sixteen years many seemed unsure as to just what the U.N. was and what it wasn't; what it could do and could not do; how it served or did not serve United States interests.

The U.N.'s major original purpose was, of course, to preserve the peace. It did not, however, have the power to preserve the peace between big nations; the big nations saw to that by insisting, the United States as well as the Soviet Union, on the right to veto action by its principal organ, the Security Council.

What happened, instead, is that the United States and the U.S.S.R. dealt with each other on peace and security issues outside the U.N., and the U.N. dealt with just about everything else, including the supervision, in Walter Lippmann's words, of "the troubles which arise from the death agony of the old empires and the birth pains of the successor states." Meanwhile, the Soviet Union used its veto so often in the Security Council that in 1951 the United States successfully sponsored the right of the General Assembly to deal with peace and security if the Security Council did not, and the membership of the General Assembly grew from 51 to 104 by the end of 1961.

The Security Council and the General Assembly were often in crisis. Crisis, of course, was their business. The U.N., naturally, reflected the cold war and all the revolutionary currents that swirled around it. And the U.N. developed a habit of surviving recurrent crisis. It did not bring Utopia but it was tougher than most people thought.

The story of the United Nations in its first decade and a half is essentially the story of Soviet efforts to restrict its role to a debating society and to prevent the organization from acquiring a capacity for executive action in response to votes of a majority of its members. This was consistent with the Soviet view of political realities, of a world in which there are only two powers, or two groups of powers, represented in the NATO and Warsaw military pacts. The rest of the world counts for nothing on a set of scales which weighs only military power. And common action among nations for economic and social progress does violence to the Communist scheme of things.

It is clear from the record that what the Soviet Union has wanted from the beginning is a United Nations which can act only if the United States and the Soviet Union are in accord. To this end it had, by the end of 1961, used its veto nearly one hundred times in the Security Council. And when a way was found around the Security Council veto, the Russians set out to paralyze the U.N. by introducing the veto into the work of the Secretariat.

The capacity of the U.N. to prevent Soviet intervention in the Congo in 1960 so infuriated Mr. Khrushchev that he spent six whole weeks away from the Kremlin to beat his fist and wave his shoe at the United Nations, to lead a personal attack on Secretary General Hammarskjöld, and to try to stampede the members into replacing him with a three-headed Secretariat. One head would speak for Moscow and its satellites, one for the United States and its friends, and one for the so-called "neutral" bloc—and each would have a veto. The neutrals were to be let in as a matter of political courtesy. It would not matter: one veto is enough. But the members did not buy it, nor did they buy it a year later when Mr. Hammarskjöld's death forced the "troika" issue to a showdown.

Against the Soviet version of a debating forum, then, the U.N. proceeded to create and protect against Soviet attack a capacity for executive action. How good was its record, bearing in mind that the U.N. is the last haven for unsolved problems and that controversies go there when nobody knows what else to do with them?

On issues of peace and security, the record shows that the U.N. has not been able in all cases to prevent the use of force and violence. France ignored a U.N. resolution calling for a pull-back of French forces in Bizerte. The Soviet Union ignored a resolution against the detonation of a fifty-megaton bomb; India ignored a resolution to call off the invasion of Goa. The record also shows that the U.N. called on the United States to lead a U.N. defense of Korea against Communist invasion . . . obtained a cease-fire in the dispute between India and Pakistan over Kashmir . . . secured an armistice in the Arab-Israeli war . . . intervened in the Suez war by obtaining a cease-fire and pull-back of forces, then put in a truce observation team which five years later was still patrolling the Gaza strip and the head of the Gulf of 'Aqaba . . . established U.N. "presences" in other trouble spots to keep an eye on explosive points . . . used mediation, conciliation, and personal diplomacy behind the scenes in a number of disputes . . . and finally mounted a major military force as the only alternative to civil war and big-power intervention in the Congo—proving at last that it could, in fact, mobilize, supply, and command troops in the field for peacekeeping missions under emergency conditions.

On colonial issues in the wake of the nationalist revolutions, the record shows that the U.N. was the scene of great emotionalism, of intemperate speeches, of hot-head debate. The open rostrum is always home to the demagogue. But the record also shows that the U.N. was serving as a "school of political responsibility," that passions were cooling, if slowly, and that the U.N. Trusteeship Council itself was a major midwife in working out the peaceful transfer to independence of seven former dependencies held in trust by its members. In 1962 the Trusteeship Council was getting toward the bottom of its agenda, its remaining business dominated by Pacific islands held in trust by the United States.

On matters concerning the revolution of rising expectations, the record shows that the U.N. had developed an array of executive agencies and programs far beyond anything foreseen in its early days, an array which, by 1961, included:

Four regional economic commissions, compiling and analyzing regional data . . . guiding national governments . . . helping with economic planning . . . sponsoring regional markets and regional development projects . . . beginning in Africa the first comprehensive resource survey of a continent big enough to contain the United States, India, and Europe, with room left over for the United Kingdom and Japan.

Specialized agencies, for health, agriculture, atomic energy, weather, labor, air transport, maritime services, investment lending, currency stabilization, and education, culture, and science. Among other things, they were running a world-wide campaign to wipe malaria from the face of the earth . . . plotting the first world-wide weather reporting system . . . running a crash program of primary education in the Congo . . . establishing the world's first food bank . . . investing in the power, transport, and other underpinnings of modern economies in the developing world . . . stabilizing trade and currency exchange rates . . . searching for new sources of cheap energy . . . granting international fellowship for research and study . . . convening international conferences of experts . . . and doing the endless donkey work of collecting data, defining terms, standardizing definitions, devising codes and regulations to help bring order to the nonpolitical business of the world community.

Executive agencies of the Secretariat, which, among other things, were caring for refugees in Palestine and elsewhere . . . providing 2,500 technicians in 1960 to some 135 countries and territories . . . helping to finance over 125 "preinvestment" projects in 43 countries, mainly in the form of resource surveys, research stations, and training institutes . . . bringing help in 1960 to 55,000,000 children and nursing mothers . . . examining 75,000,000 children for the yaws at an average of fifteen cents each and treating 27,000,000 of them at a cost of seventy-five cents apiece . . . and recruiting senior officials to work in the governments of the developing countries.

Special programs, including the Geophysical Year, which brought 30,000 scientists from 66 nations to thousands of scientific stations in a spectacular international research program in topography, geology, oceanography, seismology, meteorology, hydrology and volcanology, and a planned conference in 1963 to look at the prospects of mobilizing science and technology behind economic development in poverty-ridden areas of the world.

All this went on with little or no participation by the Soviet Union, and frequently against its will. All this went on despite the cold war, despite wrangling in the Security Council and the General Assembly, despite turmoil and crisis outside. Several examples help point the contrast.

While the Security Council was failing to stop India from the use of force against Goa, a large international team of scientists was gathering for an ambitious program of research to plumb the mysteries of the Indian Ocean.

While the Organization of American States was struggling with the problem of what to do about Castro, four U.N. agencies were agreeing to join with Mexico in a massive assault on the slums of Mexico City.

While secessionist Katanga fought U.N. troops in Elizabethville, several hundred U.N. civilians were directing the vital public services of the Congo. They had somehow managed to stop starvation and prevent epidemic, to keep the basic utilities running, and to start the staggering job of training Congolese to fill the posts left vacant when Belgian technicians departed.

And while Communist guerrillas were roaming the countryside in Viet-Nam, the U.N.'s Economic Commission for Asia and the Far East was at work on what may become the greatest river valley development scheme in the world. The Mekong River runs through or along Thailand, Laos, Cambodia, and Viet-Nam. The Mekong is sluggish in dry weather and savage in flood, but it could be the backbone for prosperous agricultural economies for four of these poorest of nations. And to survey the job, two executive arms of the United Nations, six of its specialized agencies, and nine governments were co-operating under the aegis of the regional commission. While the three princes of Laos jockeyed for control of a new government, Canadian pilots flew an aerial survey of one tributary of the Mekong, while Japanese pilots did the same for another; India had contributed rain gauges, New Zealand had provided boats, Iran had turned over petroleum, the French and Americans were training technicians, and specialists were on hand from eight U.N. agencies to work on a project which might solve the economic problems of Laos if the political problems could be survived.

The record shows that the executive agencies of the U.N. have suffered the headaches of international bureaucracy, recruitment problems, and some political horseplay. Some of them were still at loose ends in 1961, and relations between them are not always so smooth or as tidy as they might be. Nevertheless, they are growing, groping their way along, painfully expanding their budgets bit by bit, and maturing in the process. Most of them were slow to find their feet, including the largely autonomous World Bank. But after an inauspicious start, the World Bank in 1961 was an established and respected $20,000,000,000 lending institution belonging to sixty-eight governments. Its bonds were bought up by private banks and its facilities and services could provide hard loans and soft loans to governments and private enterprise, technical assistance, economic surveys, planning services, management guidance for the establishment of national development banks and, incidentally, an advanced institute for senior economic and financial officers of the less-developed countries.

In 1960 Dag Hammarskjöld addressed the U.N.'s Economic and Social Council in Geneva and pointed to a "remarkable phenomenon."

"Born as an instrument for international diplomacy," he said, "the United Nations has grown into an operational agency of significant dimensions."

This was not in line with Soviet objectives for the United Nations, or the cold war.

The Private Tide

If there was groping toward a world community at the regional and global levels of government, there was also a spilling out over national frontiers by private agencies in the postwar world. Business, finance, and management associations as well as labor unions, farm organizations, cooperatives, churches of all denominations, universities and professional societies, voluntary agencies and private foundations—all were becoming operationally involved in wider communities of action, largely indifferent to the course of cold war.

By the late 1950s, 99 out of the 100 largest United States corporations had major stakes abroad, and so did their millions of stockholders. More than 180 American universities had some kind of overseas program; 58 of them had contracts to work with foreign universities in 37 countries.

The churches were spending over $300,000,000 abroad, less and less of it for the good of heathen souls and more and more of it for the good of their material welfare.

Fifty-eight voluntary agencies were registered with the government as operators of overseas programs.

Private foundations were up to their ears in operations abroad, on which they were spending some $50,000,000 annually, some of it was for cultural affairs, but much more, for economic, educational, and social affairs.

And while the United States Government was represented in 1960 in more than four hundred official international conferences, private citizens took part in uncounted thousands of international gatherings.

As the decade of the 1960s began, about one out of every hundred Americans went to bed every night in some other country, not counting tourists. Over half of them were soldiers, sailors, or airmen. A handful were expatriates. But the rest had been swept abroad to live and work by the freshets of international community which ran at crosscurrent to the arms race and cold war, and in the same sea of history with the nationalist revolution and the revolution of rising expectations.

In the broader reality that surrounds the cold war, the record then shows that in the postwar world:

—*While the European empires came apart, their centers came together.*

—*The whole Atlantic area moved toward internal integration and external cohesion.*

—*New economic communities were aborning in major areas of the non-Communist world.*

—*Despite the Soviet Union, the United Nations developed an operational capacity for dealing with threats to the peace.*

—*Despite the Soviet Union, the United Nations created an executive capacity to promote economic and social growth.*

—*And despite the cold war, private organizations were knitting away at the fabric of world community.*

PART FOUR

COLD WAR AND FREE COMMUNITY

CHAPTER TEN

"A Mood of Temperate Optimism"

The year 1961 was a year of unrelieved crisis and tension. The new Administration in Washington inherited the stalemate of a decade and a half of cold war, together with its accumulated trouble spots. And new crises were in the making. In his inaugural address, President Kennedy warned the nation that the news could get worse before it got better. It did.

The Administration was thrown off its early stride by the disaster in Cuba's Bay of Pigs. In the remaining months of 1961 the new government was faced with Mr. Khrushchev's belligerent attitude at his meeting with the President in Vienna. It was faced with the newest and toughest revival of the Berlin crisis, leading to the eerie wall through the middle of the city. It was faced with an apparent threat of Communist conquest of Laos and large-scale Communist guerrilla warfare in Viet-Nam, with the endless dangers of the Congo affair, with the crisis in the United Nations upon the death of Secretary General Hammarskjöld in an air crash in Africa. The United States was confronted as well with the resumption of Soviet nuclear testing in the atmosphere, with the agonized impasse between the French and the Algerian nationalists, and with a new crisis between France and Tunisia over the French naval base in Bizerte. It had to deal with the first open debate in United Nations on the admission of Red China, with the Indian invasion of Goa, with the threatened Indonesian invasion of Dutch West Guinea, a rebellion in Angola, and a feud between Pakistan and Afganistan. And it was witness to a nip-and-tuck struggle of succession in the Dominican Republic after the assassination of Rafael Trujillo and a threatened civil war in Brazil after the resignation of President Janio Quadros. In the course of the same year the first conference of non-aligned states was held in Belgrade; and the Twenty-second Congress of the Communist Party of the U.S.S.R. convened in Moscow to unveil its new party program, and to reopen the wounds of de-Stalinization.

In this general climate, perhaps it should not be surprising that something like hysteria broke out in the summer of 1961 when a disaffected Cuban living in New York, then an American ex-convict, and finally an Algerian painter from Greenwich Village successively hijacked American airliners with intent to sell them to Fidel Castro. The press generally went overboard, and so did several members of Congress.

But on the next to the last day of 1961, Secretary of State Dean Rusk addressed the annual meeting of the American Historical Association in Washington and reported that, after a year in office, he was in "a mood of temperate optimism."

During that year, without fanfare, United States foreign policy underwent subtle but important changes. At least six elements added up to a basic transformation.

First, the United States began to practice twin lines of policy simultaneously. Against Communist pressure, the line was "negative." Toward opportunities elsewhere, the line was "positive." On the negative side, the United States beefed up both conventional and nonconventional military defense. It "stood firm" in Berlin, putting on shows of military force, backed by a call-up of Reservists. It supported a counter-guerrilla campaign in Viet-Nam. It opposed successfully the admission of Communist China to the United Nations. It accepted the challenge of an all-out race to the moon.

But simultaneously, the United States proposed a comprehensive general disarmament plan. It spelled out proposals to reserve outer space for peaceful uses. It offered to cooperate internationally in the development and use of weather and communication satellite systems. It urged the improvement of U.N. machinery for the settlement of disputes and the supervision of peaceful change. And it established the world's first official agency to work full-time on systems of arms control and disarmament.

Thus United States policy was to react by standing firm in cases where the Communists had a natural monopoly on initiative, and to move ahead everywhere else by independent initiatives. "Defensive" and "progressive," "negative" and "positive" postures, it turned out, are not mutually exclusive. The trick was not to be diverted from United States initiative by a fixation with initiatives from the other side.

Second, the United States learned to deal simultaneously with all major areas of the world, regardless of the location of the most pressing current crisis or threat. Policy faced east, west, and south at the same time. It was no longer a question of whether attention should be focused on Europe, or the Western Hemisphere, or Asia and Africa, or somewhere else. For if Europe is neglected, the center of free world power is neglected; if Latin America is ignored, the Western Hemisphere is vulnerable; if Asia and Africa are left to drift away, there is little chance of defending Europe. The job was to weld together the free societies in the Northern Hemisphere and, at the same time, build strong bridges between the Northern and Southern Hemisphere.

Thus the United States did not concentrate all its attention on building the Atlantic Community, or on the Western Hemisphere, or on a new relationship with Japan, or on support for economic and social progress in Africa or Southeast Asia. It did all these at once in a world which had become so interdependent that it was no longer safe to ignore any part of it, even if a crisis in a particular place was dominating the headlines. Like it or not, what happens in one place has its repercussions everywhere else.

Third, the United States came to regard the several channels of diplomacy and the several levels of international organization, not as alternative avenues for foreign policy, but as a spectrum of complementary instruments. Important negotiations, particularly those of deepest interest to the great powers, were conducted through nation-to-nation diplomatic channels. In NATO, and in OAS and the OECD, the United States worked diplomatically within the structure of alliances dealing both with internal relations among the members and with common policy toward other countries. From the outside, the United States also lent diplomatic support to the emerging economic communities of which it was not a member. And in the United Nations, the United States was up to its ears in the newer arts of parliamentary diplomacy within a near-universal organization.

The different levels of organization and the different types of diplomacy each had their strengths and weaknesses. One would be more suitable than the others to a particular problem or opportunity. But over a range of problems and opportunities, the instruments and techniques were now seen as a spectrum of useful tools. None offer the answer to everything. All are subject to improvement, but none are dispensable. Sponsorship of a growing community in the North Atlantic is not an alternative to full support of the United

Nations; an open debate in the General Assembly does not reduce the value of quiet diplomacy; and U.S. association with regionalism in one area is not an alternative to association with regionalism in some other area.

For these reasons, the U.S. sought to work simultaneously at the nation-to-nation, at the regional, and at the universal level; and it practiced bilateral, multilateral, and parliamentary diplomacy at one and the same time.

Fourth, the United States gave up the notion that the trouble with the world is a pesky series of crises which have to be dealt with temporarily on a crash basis, one at a time. Instead, it was taken for granted that the spot crises were related events of a world in which rapid and often violent change had become normal. So the U.S. began to organize foreign operations on a long-term basis. The Agency for International Development was authorized for the first time to plan ahead for more than a twelve-month period. It also began to do research on economic and technical aid and the process of economic and social growth, for which much had been spent but about which little was known. In Latin America, the Alliance for Progress was established on a ten-year basis. At the United Nations, the U.S. sponsored a Decade of Development to guide U.N. assistance programs into the decade of the 1970s. In the Atlantic area, the OECD worked out goals for economic growth for the rest of the decade.

Fifth, the United States began to direct its overseas aid programs to the long-range task of nation-building. An immediate Communist threat was no longer the sole qualification for American assistance. The new criteria were based on willingness of local governments to make the effort and mount the reforms needed to build the kind of future society which is invulnerable to subversion from any source. The negative, defensive, exclusively anti-Communist flavor of U.S. aid programs since the Truman Doctrine was beginning to fade. The psychological price of the containment policy was about paid off. U.S. objectives were now expressed in aid toward land reform, progressive taxation, better housing and health for entire populations.

The U.S. was shedding the role of defender of the *status quo*. Feudal landowners, reactionary politicians, and usurious moneylenders were now seen as co-enemies, along with the Communists, of U.S. objectives in newly developing lands. The U.S. had returned to the original doctrine of the Marshall Plan, to a policy directed "not against any party or doctrine but against hunger, poverty, desperation and chaos." And the U.S. was beginning to pay more attention to the fact that one dollar invested in economic development produces at best only one dollar's worth of results—unless it trains people and builds institutions to multiply the product. So the U.S. was turning more toward the job of helping to build institutions which can carry on after aid is withdrawn, which can guide social change, and which underpin the fabric of modern societies. Peace Corps workers on community development projects were one step in this direction. Guidance in the establishment of development centers in Latin America was another. Help in organizing rural co-operatives, technical institutes, universities, and other institutions reflected the new pattern. If the trend continues, it seems likely that a widening segment of private American organizations would become involved directly in nation-building abroad.

Sixth, the permanent themes of Communist propaganda were losing their cutting edge. For all its variants, Communist propaganda over the years has had two effective *anti* themes and one effective *pro* theme. The *anti* themes are "imperialism" and "capitalism." The *pro* theme is "peace." Other standbys of Communist propaganda, like "democracy," and other techniques, like "foreign aid," are stolen or copied from the Western world, and most people know it.

But in early 1962 the "imperialism" theme was losing some of its potency, for the simple reason that the Western empires were in the last stage of dismemberment. The United States provided unflagging support of the U.N. operation in the Congo. It supported moderate Asian-African resolutions on colonial issues in the General Assembly in 1961. There was little credibility left in the Communist pretension that the U.S. belonged in the "imperialist" camp. Indeed, there was not much left of the camp at all. And as noted earlier, the time seemed at hand when the sin of colonialism could now be pinned on the Soviet Union.

Meanwhile, "capitalism" was losing its standing as a dirty word. Many of the new countries began independence with tight restrictions against the participation of foreign private capital in their economic development. Within a few years most of them had a change of heart. They found, after all, that private investment from overseas could play a useful role. Regulations and legislation were changed in a large number of countries to encourage the flow of foreign capital into useful projects. Missions were sent to the United States to promote private U.S. investment in Asia and Africa. Communist propaganda could get less mileage out of anticapitalism slogans.

Ever since World War II the Communist propaganda apparatus labored, long and expensively, and sometimes with distressing success, to establish monopoly on the word "peace." The "general and complete disarmament" called for by Mr. Khrushchev was better propaganda than an unconvincing U.S. offer to discuss "first steps." But during the first half of 1961 the United States was in a position to press hard for Soviet signature of a treaty to ban atomic testing. When the Soviets, instead, launched a long series of atmospheric tests, there was not much left in the "peace" line for Soviet propaganda. A few months later the U.S. dropped its coyness about general disarmament, presented a credible program for the complete elimination of all armed forces capable of waging international war, and urged the Soviet Union to get on with negotiations. The United States was gaining the initiative over the Soviet Union on the issue of peace. China could do no better than Russia with peace propaganda, since Mao endorsed the Soviet resumption of tests, trained guerrillas to overthrow other people's governments, and hewed to the line that political power comes out of the barrel of a gun.

By the beginning of 1962, then, the hardy perennials of Communist propaganda were dead or fading. It remained for the Communists to try to persuade other nations that Communism is a short cut to a modern industrial society. But the rest of the world was wide open to inspection on this point. And the economic performance of Germany, Italy, Japan, Israel, Mexico, Puerto Rico, and others suggested that Communism is not an exclusive formula for rapid economic development.

The Grand Design

Mr. Rusk's mood of "temperate optimism" at the turn of the year might, then, be compounded of two factors: the record of fifteen years of cold war in its larger setting and the trend of United States foreign policy.

The record of world affairs in the first and second stages of the cold war showed that the aggressive outward thrust of Soviet Communism had been contained for twelve years. It showed that the world communist movement no longer had a single center, and Red China was in serious economic straits. It showed that the new nations had a passionate attachment to independence and a surprising resistance to Communist subversion; and that the Western world was caught up in a powerful movement toward unity and prosperity, while regionalism was growing elsewhere. And it showed that the United Nations had developed a capacity to conduct major peace-keeping operations and growing programs of economic and technical assistance.

The record of recent trends in United States foreign policy showed that the U.S. now had a policy that was defensive toward the Communist world and progressive everywhere else. It was dealing at one and the same time with all major areas of the world. It was working at bilateral, regional, and multilateral diplomacy simultaneously. It was organizing its operations on a long-term basis, and beginning to associate its own objectives with the aspirations of peoples instead of the exasperations of their leaders. In short, the United States was beginning to export its most valuable assets—liberal ideas and flexible institutions which can absorb and guide change without violent explosions.

Taken together, the accumulated shifts in U.S. policy were beginning to etch out a grand design for a new world order, an alternative goal to a Communist one world. For the first time since Communism gained control of Russia, another political system consciously accepted social change and deliberately adopted social goals for the world at large.

Both designs—communist and free world—held out security and personal welfare for masses of people. One offered to work toward the goal by consent; the other, by coercion. One cast up a drab, gray world of boring uniformity; the other, a world of bright diversity.

The grand design emerging from U.S. policy was a world of overlapping communities of free and independent nations, each following its own bent but each joined in voluntary associations of widening membership in common pursuit of a more decent standard of life. World uniformity, stamped from *anyone's* mold, is the least likely of all outcomes for a world of such cultural, racial, national, and personal diversity. For this reason, the free world design was not only more attractive but also a much more workable one.

At last there appeared a "better idea" than communism to contest for the "mind of man." As 1962 got under way, then, it appeared that time, if well used, would be working on the side of the Community of the Free.

CHAPTER ELEVEN

"The Most Dangerous Period"

Despite the record of cold war and Communism, there were people in this country in early 1962 who still believed, or at least claimed, that the United States "lost" China to the Communists. Despite the record, there were those who believed that a government in Africa which accepts foreign aid from Czechoslovakia is "down the drain," and that a government in Asia which owns a steel mill is on the slippery slope to communism.

As this is written, an American general who was relieved of his command is telling audiences that the United States has surrendered its sovereignty completely to the United Nations. And Right Wing groups of frightened citizens are telling each other that the dark agents of Communism have penetrated the innards of American government, the trade unions, the educational system, the courts, and all but the fundamentalist churches.

There was nothing new in the spectacle of zealots consumed with belief that all the troubles of the Republic are due to a sinister band of conspirators. As Arthur Schlesinger, Jr., said in a speech in January 1962:

> In the 1820s, honest men tried to save us from the conspiracy of the Masons. In the 1850s, the Know-Nothings tried to save us from the immigrant conspiracy. In the 1890s, the American Protective Association tried to save us from a

> conspiracy of Catholics and Jews and Negroes. In the thirties, the American Liberty League tried to save us from the radicals. In the forties, the America First Committee tried to save us from the interventionists. And today the John Birch Society tries to save us from the graduated income tax, Chief Justice Warren, the fluoridation of water and the twentieth century.

But the John Birch Society is not responsible for the alarming comments quoted in the first chapter of this book. Despite the record of the cold war set forth in the subsequent chapters, at least some respectable opinion leaders had persuaded themselves that we are "losing" the cold war, and that "total defeat" may be just around the corner.

Leaving aside the hysteria—and the politics—of the radical Right, there are a number of reasons which might explain American frustration in the bewildering world of cold war.

First, we are victims of our own history, which has taught us that we are the sole masters of our own destiny. Now, as Robert Heilbroner has put it: ". . . we have emerged into an open sea where powerful contrary winds come directly into conflict with our passage." Our history did not prepare us well to live in a world of "contrary winds."

Second, we are accustomed to an either-or system of values. Things are either good or bad, black or white, right or wrong, stupid or intelligent. This is poor training for coming to grips with a world of grays in which decisions must be taken on many-sided issues, necessarily leading to mixed results—some "good," some "bad."

Third, we instinctively believe that if there is a "problem," there must, by definition, be a "solution," as though most of us in our private lives had not learned to live with problems indefinitely, precisely because there is no solution. And as though every "solution" may not raise the next "problem."

Fourth, we tend to look for simple remedies to the woes which beset us. This lends credence to the conspiracy theory of history, and to its cheap-and-easy answers.

Fifth, we are stuck with a military vocabulary to describe the struggle between "democracy" and "communism," both of which we strongly assume to be fixed and unchanging absolutes. Since the cold war is directed by "strategies" and "tactics" and is fought with various "weapons" on many "fronts," it is recorded almost daily that, in this or that encounter, we have won a "victory" or suffered a "defeat." No one points out that if either side could have his own way, there could be no stalemate; indeed, the cold war could not exist at all. And reporters and analysts of cold war have a curious tendency to accumulate the "defeats" and forget the "victories"—thus adding to the public impression of steady retreat before the invincible forces of communism.

Thus, our own history, our habits of thought, our approach to "problems," our search for simple solutions, and the very words we use to describe struggle could all contribute to a sense of frustration after fifteen years of unyielding cold war and chaotic events, many of which we could influence, but few of which we could control. Frustration can, theoretically, inspire a determined new effort, if new direction is found as an outlet for constructive energy. But it also can inspire either apathy or belligerence; and either could be fatal if it became the predominant mood of the nation.

Perhaps this was in President Kennedy's mind when he

remarked at a press conference in 1961 that we are passing through "the most dangerous period in history." The President did not elaborate. But certainly there was no shortage of dangers. The greatest of these dangers lay in the direct confrontation of the great powers with each other. But some of them lay outside these relations. And others were internal to the great powers.

In the early days of 1962 four ominous and related questions hung in the balance, insisting on answers.

Would the nuclear arms race spiral into another round of frantic competition?

Would nuclear arms capacity spread from four nations to five, six, ten or more?

Would outer space be reserved for peaceful uses, or left for competitive exploitation for military advantage?

Would some way be found out of fifteen years of deadlock in Berlin?

President Kennedy alone could decide whether the national security requires a resumption of United States testing of atomic weapons in the atmosphere. If no halt can be brought to the fitful race to catch up, or get ahead, or stay ahead, each side will simply continue to build up bigger or better or more versatile arsenals of nuclear weapons. The scientists say that there is no foreseeable limit to the size of the bang that can be stuffed into a thermonuclear warhead.

At the same time it seemed to be up to the great powers to come to agreement if they want to stop the spread of nuclear weapons from one country to the next. And one of the next almost surely would be Communist China. According to the National Planning Association, six or eight nations have the scientific capacity to produce nuclear weapons, and more will acquire it. Without big power agreement on international elimination or control of nuclear weapons, there seemed little practical hope of evading what the National Planning Association called "the nth Country problem."

There would not be much time to answer these questions. Nor could the decision on outer space be long postponed. No one in the free world could know what would follow the Soviet's man-in-orbit. But the United States was on the verge of launching a system of communications and weather satellite systems, and it could be assumed that the Russians, sooner or later, could have a variety of electronic gear in regular orbit around the earth.

As these questions hung in the balance at the beginning of 1962 the United States Ambassador in Moscow was engaged in probing discussions with the Soviet Foreign Minister to see if some basis could be found for a negotiated settlement in Berlin. For three years Mr. Khrushchev had insisted that he was on the verge of signing a separate peace treaty with Herr Ulbricht's regime in East Germany, thus turning over to the German Communists control of Western access to the German capital. In 1958 he laid down a six-month ultimatum, and then let it pass in favor of a Summit Conference. Early in 1961 he said that the thing must be done before the year was out. Then he fuzzed the deadline, and let it pass again. In the meantime, there were provocations and probings from the Soviet side. There were rejoinders and shows of strength from the Western side. The refugees fled. The wall went up. Convoys moved conspicuously through the corridor to West Berlin. American officials delayed in East Berlin were recovered by American armed guards and escorted across the line. And for a while the Russian and American tanks pulled up within a few yards of each other. When the original deadline came at the end of the year, the test of wills was in stalemate. On the Berlin issue as such, there was not much more room for diplomatic maneuver in Moscow than for military maneuver on Friederichstraase.

Mr. Khrushchev had insisted, at the risk of dividing the Communist world, that nuclear war must be ruled out as a means of settling international dispute. The United States was committed never to strike first with nuclear weapons. President Kennedy assured the world before the United Nations that the United States had elaborate precautions against accidental release of an atomic explosion, and he offered to share safety technology with other nations.

At the beginning of 1962 the United States and Russia were entering the eighth month of a joint effort to convince the feuding princes of Laos to agree on a formula for an independent, neutral Laos. But both sides were still adamant about what each considered its vital interests in Berlin. Armed forces faced each other on the spot. Passion was separated from despair only by an ugly and provocative wall of cement and barbed wire. Only a thin lifeline to Western Berlin ran through Communist-held territory, and missiles sat on their pads, armed with thermonuclear warheads.

The test of wills in Berlin, from the middle through the end of 1961, was played out with cool heads in tight control on both sides. But there was always the off-chance of a miscalculation, of a human error. The misreading of a sudden blip on a radar screen, an order by a trigger-happy officer, a shot by a nervous young sentry, a false intelligence report —these or other errors of fallible men conceivably could set the nuclear powers on the ultimate collision course. As Donald Michael of the Brookings Institution has commented: "Short tempers do not even out."

In the fall of 1961 President Kennedy addressed the General Assembly of the United Nations. He challenged the Soviet Union to join the United States in a "peace race." He outlined a comprehensive American program for general disarmament. He called for projection of the rule of law into outer space to reserve it for peaceful uses. And he insisted that machinery for peaceful settlement of international disputes be built up as the machinery of war is torn down.

In the course of 1962 the world would know whether it was condemned to live in indefinite terror of an onrushing nuclear arms race, perhaps projected into outer space. United Nations commissions on both disarmament and outer space were scheduled to meet in the spring to take fresh starts at American initiative. Time for maneuver and propaganda was running out. Until a corner is turned toward control of nuclear weapons, nuclear war could not be ruled out as an impossibility in early 1962. If the danger was remote, it was, nonetheless, the ultimate danger.

But the Soviet Union and the United States were not the only parties at dispute in the beginning of 1962. The missile race between them was not the only arms race going on in the world. Berlin and Laos were not the only spots of crisis.

As the new year came in, there was an armistice but no peace settlement between Israel and the Arab states. There was a cease-fire but no settlement between India and Pakistan in their dispute over Kashmir. Pakistan and Afghanistan had closed their borders. Cambodia had just broken diplomatic relations with Thailand and Viet-Nam. And Indonesia was threatening to invade Dutch New Guinea.

The world of 1962 inherited all the unsolved disputes of the ages. Many of them were not between great powers, but the great powers were deeply involved with the security and politics of the last corner of earth. Thus a tribal war in the Khyber Pass or in the province of Katanga could spark reaction in Moscow and Washington.

And even if stability comes to the Congo, even if the colonies of Portugal are set on the road to freedom, the brooding issue of "white supremacy" hangs over Northern Rhodesia and haunts South Africa. It seems to be easier for a government to agree to give up a colony than for a settler to agree to give in to majority rule. Atomic weapons are not needed for massacres, but massacres could "escalate," too.

The record of cold war since the time of Korea suggests that Mr. Khrushchev is impressed by the danger that "limited war" could not be kept limited to conventional forces. He has even professed that revolution is "not for export" and that Communism might come to power in some places by parliamentary means.

But he has always left open the possibility, even the duty, of Communist support for "just wars of liberation." This could mean outside support for Communist-led insurrections against non-Communist governments, which the United States might feel compelled to support. The mighty Communist military machines would thus be limited to the undignified role of smuggling small arms across frontiers and training guerrillas for "internal war." But that is just what the Chinese were doing for Laos, Viet-Nam, and others. It was another danger of the age.

In the world of new nations, there was still another, more general kind of danger. The struggle which goes on in Asia, Africa, and Latin America is essentially a race to build modern societies. This race has been made possible by exploding technology; it owes nothing to communism.

But Mr. Khrushchev has said officially to the assembled Russian Party that Communism will triumph because others voluntarily will copy the Soviet system, which lifted Russia from degrading poverty to a modern society within a single generation. There is not much truth in that picture, but just enough to make it seductive.

There is also the possibility that foreign capital will not be available in sufficient quantities to finance a satisfactory rate of economic development in the emerging countries. The only alternative is to create the capital by forced savings, which means lowering already low standards of living. And that, in turn, requires an authoritarian political system.

But there is another danger that would open special opportunities for the Communists. It is the possibility of social breakdown. Nations in the process of rapid change have to abandon the old institutions which kept order in the old society. If new institutions do not take their place, social anarchy could lead to political breakdown, the precise conditions under which armed Communists have been able to take power in other countries.

Thus the difference between evolution and revolution in the nations racing to catch up with the twentieth century may well turn on the ability of public and private institutions to direct and absorb rapid change. This means more than armed forces and militia. It means housing departments, health departments, water departments, sewer departments, municipal courts, and all the institutional paraphernalia to service the booming populations of cities in the wake of industrialization, for the rootless and miserable alley dweller is the basic unit of the street mob. It means research stations, extension services, credit systems, and rural road departments. It is not enough to teach modern farm practices to a handful of farmers without building the organizations needed by modern agriculture. It means business and trade associations, professional societies, research facilities, and a career civil service to absorb the talents of the newly educated, for unemployed intellectuals are the most dangerous animals on earth.

Static societies openly invite revolution. But rapidly modernizing societies can invite the kind of social-political breakdown which opens the door to communism if they do not create new institutions of order to replace the ones they abandon.

The record shows that Communist propaganda, infiltration, subversion, and other "weapons" have not succeeded in bringing down national states without superior military power available to the Communists. It also shows that Communist parties have lost important support in important places in recent years, and are in general disarray elsewhere. But the final Communist talent is that of the scavenger. In a world of violent change, social disruption, ancient feuds, widespread injustice, and political inexperience, the potential capacity of the Communist parties to add to their record as scavengers cannot be ignored.

High among the dangers of the period was the threat of frustration within the superpowers. The possibility that this could give rise to either apathy or belligerence in the United States already has been mentioned.

Perhaps there is comfort in the fact that the Communist bloc is not the monolithic structure it was supposed to be. Perhaps it is reassuring to know that the Communist world no longer has a single ideological center. It is gratifying to see evidence that the urge to national independence has not died in the satellite states. And there is always hope that better things may come out of political disagreements within the parties that rule the Communist states.

But serious hostility between Russia and China carries unknowable risks to the peace of the world. Another "Hungary," though physically unlikely, would pose an excruciating problem for the free world. And a serious internal struggle for power might drive a dominant Communist clique to seek vindication in external adventure. Troubles within the Communist world are not without danger for the rest of us.

Meanwhile, Mr. Khrushchev confesses the failure of postwar Soviet policy in Europe whenever he pleads that the situation in Berlin is "abnormal." Restlessness in Eastern Europe is a constant concern of the Soviet leaders. The wall in Berlin stands as a shocking advertisement of the inhumanity of Communism and its rejection by the Germans under Communist control, while the German Federal Republic is integrated with Western Europe, allied with NATO, and a key member of an awesomely powerful Atlantic Community. Despite every device in the Soviet bag of tricks, the Western alliance has not come apart. The European empires were dissolving without benefit to Communism; a strong trend toward unification was evident in the non-Communist world; and United States policy was evolving an attractive design for pluralistic communities of freedom held together by consent. The world could not look promising from inside the Kremlin.

It is impossible to know what pressures might be put on Khrushchev from within his Party, what demands might be building up for a Communist "victory," what spurs might goad him to recklessness. But the possibility of serious frustration within the Kremlin must be counted as one of the dangers of the era.

As 1962 began, the agenda of dangers ran from nuclear

war to national frustration. It was an agenda framed by a long stalemate of the cold war powers. The contemporary era might well be termed the "most dangerous period in history."

CHAPTER TWELVE

The Third Stage of Cold War

The first stage of cold war ran from 1946 to around 1953. It was a period of Soviet expansion and American containment. In Eastern and Central Europe, the Soviet Union violated agreements and used every form of coercion and terror to bring once-independent nations under its control. In Korea Stalin tried aggression by proxy. But in the end he found he could not push outward beyond the areas occupied or significantly influenced by Soviet power on the spot at the end of World War II.

The second stage of the cold war ran from around 1953 to about the end of 1961. In this period Khrushchev abandoned Soviet isolationism to wage political warfare around the world. He tried to turn the anticolonial revolution toward Communism. He offered aid and trade to divert the revolution of rising expectations into a Communist mold. Both failed. In 1961, Khrushchev tried to assert influence by terror, exploding huge nuclear weapons and threatening small states with atomic blackmail. This failed, too.

By the beginning of 1962 it seemed clear that the cold war was entering a third stage. What it would be like, no one could tell because the Communist world was in lively and ominous ferment. The rift between Communist Russia and Communist China, which had opened about five years before, now seemed serious and probably irreparable. The second wave of de-Stalinization, launched at the Twenty-second Party Congress in 1961, seemed to be rocking the satellite states, as the first wave had rocked them in 1956. The American and British press carried long accounts of evident confusion within the Soviet Union. The lengths of in-fighting among Communist parties was almost comically illustrated by an Albanian aircraft dropping leaflets over Eastern Germany, appealing to that country's Communist rulers to act against the overlordship of Moscow. Communist parties throughout the world were in furor as China challenged Russia as the fountainhead of true communist faith. Some communist factions around the world supported Moscow. Others bucked for Peking. But most of them seemed to be headed more and more in the direction of independence from both.

Behind it all was the bitter fight among Communists over communist ideology summed up in the question: Is peaceful coexistence possible or desirable? Khrushchev said Yes. Mao said No. It seemed as if Mao were trying to push the Soviet Union into war with the United States. It was at least conceivable that he really was pushing the Soviet Union toward a *modus vivendi* with the West.

Whatever comes out of the inner conspiracies of the Communist bloc, the world at large probably will be a wild and woolly place during the new stage of cold war. Crisis will be normal. Among other predictable pieces of the picture, it seemed clear that:

—*Political, economic and social life in great areas of the world will continue in the process of disruptive change.*

—*Science will romp ahead with total disregard for the political means of coping with its wonders.*

—*Messrs. Khrushchev, Mao Tse-tung, Tito, Togliatti, Thorez, Adenauer, de Gaulle, Chiang Kai-shek,*

Franco and Salazar will, among others, pass from the scene.

—*Still more nations will enter the arena of world affairs.*

—*Political power will be diffused as several nations in Asia and Africa rise to big-power status.*

—*"Imperialism" will pass from the scene.*

—*"Neutrality" will remain in vogue among presently uncommitted states and tug at the policies of some which are now committed.*

—*Novel political systems and mixed economies will defy existing labels.*

—*Politics will reign supreme in the first era of mass politics in a world in which freedom is as hard to hold as it is to come by.*

All this suggests that the American public is in for a period of contradictions, ironies, paradoxes, and crises, which will offer a tough test of its nerve and maturity. It also suggests that the world of the third stage of cold war will be one of vast diversity, of pluralism compounded. The evolving societies of the hundred-plus nations of the world will not be very much like the present society of the Soviet Union nor the present society of the United States, both of which happen to be changing also.

When and how the new communities of the free world would outlast the community of coercion, no man could say. In the last analysis, as others have noted, there is no last analysis of history. In the end, then, political judgment is subjective: it is personal optimism or personal pessimism which tips the scale between faith and frustration.

At the beginning of 1962 concrete factors weighed heavily on the side of faith in the Community of the Free: the military might and the unparalleled economy of the United States; the far-flung range of military alliances embracing forty-odd allies around the world; the new strengths of Europe and Japan; the shining prospect of Atlantic Community; the hopes for a closer inter-American community; and the vision of other communities of free nations linked with the United States in free consent.

But there are nonmaterial assets which also belong on the side of the free. They are not available to the side of coercion.

—*To be able to live with the Charter of the United Nations.*

—*To be able to accept international decision and to tolerate international inspection.*

—*To be able to manage the difficult business of working in free alliance with other sovereign states.*

—*To be able to co-operate, accommodate, and compromise.*

—*To be able to identify the national interest with the national interest of most other countries.*

—*To be able to support liberal evolution of open societies by democratic reform.*

—*To be able to make acts conform with words—and words with acts.*

—*To be a society which, for all its sins and pretensions, fights everlastingly for the unalienable Rights to Life, Liberty, and the pursuit of Happiness.*

These are assets which warrant, to at least one who has looked at the record of cold war, a fresh burst of faith of the Community of the Free.

DATE DUE

MAY 5	1968		
MAY 21 1968			
DEC 13	1976		
MY 10 '83			

GAYLORD

PRINTED IN U.S.A.